ALL CLEAR 2

Listening and Speaking

Helen Kalkstein Fragiadakis

Australia • Canada • Mexico • Singapore • Spain • United Kingdom • United States

All Clear 2
Listening and Speaking
Helen Kalkstein Fragiadakis

Publisher, Academic ESL: Sherrise Roehr
Consulting Editor: James W. Brown
Acquisitions Editor: Tom Jefferies
Director of Content Development: Anita Raducanu
Associate Development Editor: Katherine Carroll
Associate Development Editor: Jennifer Meldrum
Editorial Assistant: Katherine Reilly
Director of Product Marketing: Amy Mabley
Executive Marketing Manager: Jim McDonough
Senior Field Marketing Manager: Donna Lee Kennedy
Product Marketing Manager: Katie Kelley
Associate Marketing Manager: Caitlin Driscoll
Senior Production Editor: Maryellen E. Killeen
Senior Print Buyer: Betsy Donaghey
Project Manager: Tunde Dewey
Composition: Parkwood Composition
Interior Design: Lori Stuart
Artist: Steve Haefele
Printer: Edwards Brothers

Printed in the United States of America.
1 2 3 4 5 6 7 8 9 10 09 08 07

For more information contact Thomson Heinle, 25 Thomson Place, Boston, MA 02210 USA, or visit our Internet site at elt.thomson.com

ISBN 10: 1-4130-1704-5
ISBN 13: 978-1-4130-1704-5
ISE ISBN 10: 1-4130-2098-4
ISE ISBN 13: 978-1-4130-1704-5

To my family, yesterday and today—

Acknowledgments

The original *All Clear* idioms text came out more than twenty years ago, and the additional two texts at higher and lower levels appeared years later. It was always my dream for these three texts to become a comprehensive listening and speaking series using idioms and other expressions as springboards for activities, and I have many people to thank for making this dream come true.

To Sherrise Roehr, publisher, and Jim Brown, consulting editor, thank you for getting the ball rolling on this project. To editors Tom Jefferies, Katie Carroll, Jennifer Meldrum, Katherine Reilly, and Maryellen Eschmann-Killeen, thank you for all your support. To Steve Haefele, thank you for your creative and humorous art, which brings so much of *All Clear* to life. And to Tunde Dewey, my project manager, thank you so very much for your wonderfully thorough and professional work.

I would also like to express my gratitude to the many colleagues who over the years gave me extremely valuable feedback, which I incorporated into the new editions. I would especially like to thank Inocencia Dacumos, Kathi Jordan, Rosemary Loughman, Helen Munch, Kathleen Pappert, Ellen Rosenfield, and Larry Statan.

A big thank you goes to my daughter Melissa, who for years has enthusiastically given me feedback to help make the language in *All Clear* dialogues as natural as possible. Thank you, Melissa, for using your wonderful sense of *what people really say* to answer such questions as "How would you say this?", "Would you ever say that?", "Does this sound natural?", and "What's another way to say. . . ?"

I would also like to thank my many students for their interest and insightful questions as I taught with the *All Clear* texts. While teaching, I jotted down their questions in the textbook margins. And then, while revising the texts, I used their questions as guides to improve the material.

Finally, I would like to thank Michael Lewis, who has put the lexical approach in the center stage of language acquisition. I wrote the first *All Clear* in the early 1980s, and ten years later it was a revelation to hear Lewis talk about the value of teaching "chunks" of language—collocations and fixed expressions. I have found that focusing on lexical items (many, but not all of them, idiomatic) in a natural dialogue can provide concrete material that can serve as a springboard for numerous activities in a listening/speaking class. Thank you, Michael Lewis, for bringing the lexical approach to the forefront of language teaching and learning.

Helen Kalkstein Fragiadakis
March, 2007

CONTENTS

CONTENTS

CONTENTS

CONTENTS

A Walk-Through Guide

***All Clear 2—Listening and Speaking* is the second in this best-selling series of conversationally-oriented texts. High-frequency American English expressions such as *get cold feet,* and *be in the mood* are presented in meaningful contexts to develop speaking, listening, and pronunciation skills. This text is appropriate for intermediate and high-intermediate level listening/speaking, pronunciation, and vocabulary courses.**

- **Theme-based units** feature contextualized listening activities.

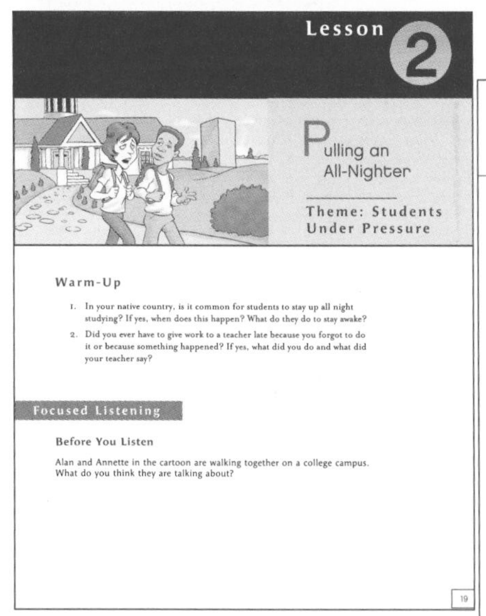

Lesson 2

Pulling an All-Nighter

Theme: Students Under Pressure

Warm-Up

1. In your native country, is it common for students to stay up all night studying? If yes, when does this happen? What do they do to stay awake?
2. Did you ever have to give work to a teacher late because you forgot to do it or because something happened? If yes, what did you do and what did your teacher say?

Focused Listening

Before You Listen

Alan and Annette in the cartoon are walking together on a college campus. What do you think they are talking about?

19

- **Focused Listening** sections feature activities before and after each conversation for increased comprehension.

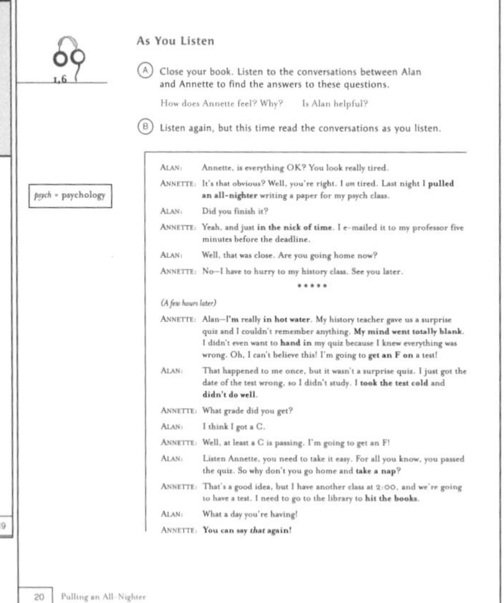

1,6

As You Listen

(A) Close your book. Listen to the conversations between Alan and Annette to find the answers to these questions.

How does Annette feel? Why? Is Alan helpful?

(B) Listen again, but this time read the conversations as you listen.

psych = psychology

ALAN: Annette, is everything OK? You look really tired.
ANNETTE: It's that obvious? Well, you're right. I *am* tired. Last night I **pulled an all-nighter** writing a paper for my psych class.
ALAN: Did you finish it?
ANNETTE: Yeah, and just **in the nick of time**. I e-mailed it to my professor five minutes before the deadline.
ALAN: Well, that was close. Are you going home now?
ANNETTE: No—I have to hurry to my history class. See you later.

* * * * *

(A few hours later)

ANNETTE: Alan—**I'm** really **in hot water**. My history teacher gave us a surprise quiz and I couldn't remember anything. **My mind went totally blank**. I didn't even want to **hand in** my quiz because I knew everything was wrong. Oh, I can't believe this! I'm going to **get an F on** a test!
ALAN: That happened to me once, but it wasn't a surprise quiz. I just got the date of the test wrong, so I didn't study. I **took the test cold** and **didn't do well**.
ANNETTE: What grade did you get?
ALAN: I think I got a C.
ANNETTE: Well, at least a C is passing. I'm going to get an F!
ALAN: Listen Annette, you need to take it easy. For all you know, you passed the quiz. So why don't you go home and **take a nap**?
ANNETTE: That's a good idea, but I have another class at 2:00, and we're going to have a test. I need to go to the library to **hit the books**.
ALAN: What a day you're having!
ANNETTE: **You can say *that* again!**

20 Pulling an All-Nighter

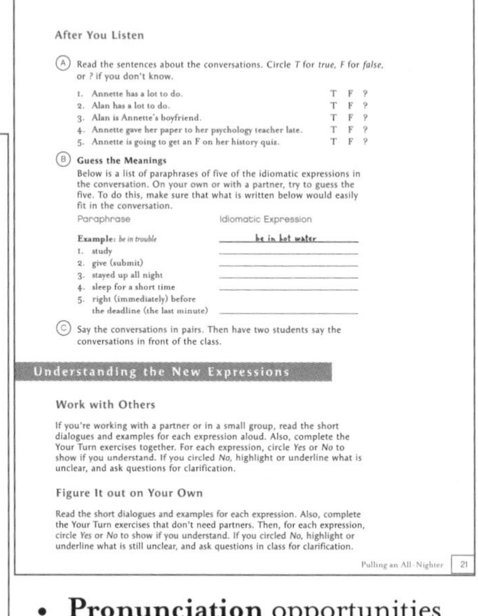

After You Listen

(A) Read the sentences about the conversations. Circle *T* for *true, F* for *false*, or *?* if you don't know.

1. Annette has a lot to do. T F ?
2. Alan has a lot to do. T F ?
3. Alan is Annette's boyfriend. T F ?
4. Annette gave her paper to her psychology teacher late. T F ?
5. Annette is going to get an F on her history quiz. T F ?

(B) **Guess the Meanings**
Below is a list of paraphrases of five of the idiomatic expressions in the conversation. On your own or with a partner, try to guess the five. To do this, make sure that what is written below would easily fit in the conversation.

Paraphrase	Idiomatic Expression
Example: *be in trouble*	be in hot water
1. study	________
2. give (submit)	________
3. stayed up all night	________
4. sleep for a short time	________
5. right (immediately) before the deadline (the last minute)	________

(C) Say the conversations in pairs. Then have two students say the conversations in front of the class.

Understanding the New Expressions

Work with Others

If you're working with a partner or in a small group, read the short dialogues and examples for each expression aloud. Also, complete the Your Turn exercises together. For each expression, circle *Yes* or *No* to show if you understand. If you circled *No,* highlight or underline what is unclear, and ask questions for clarification.

Figure It out on Your Own

Read the short dialogues and examples for each expression. Also, complete the Your Turn exercises that don't need partners. Then, for each expression, circle *Yes* or *No* to show if you understand. If you circled *No,* highlight or underline what is still unclear, and ask questions in class for clarification.

Pulling an All-Nighter 21

- **Pronunciation** opportunities in every lesson allow students to practice conversation skills in context and with new vocabulary.

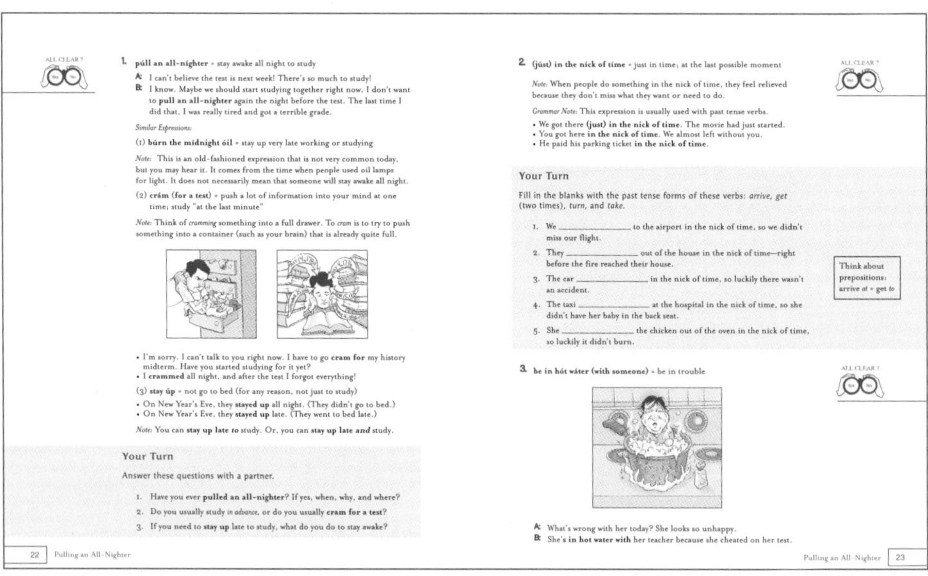

ALL CLEAR?

1. **púll an all-níghter** = stay awake all night to study

A: I can't believe the test is next week! There's so much to study!
B: I know. Maybe we should start studying together right now. I don't want to **pull an all-nighter** again the night before the test. The last time I did that, I was really tired and got a terrible grade.

Similar Expressions:

(1) **búrn the mídnight óil** = stay up very late working or studying

Note: This is an old-fashioned expression that is not very common today, but you may hear it. It comes from the time when people used oil lamps for light. It does not necessarily mean that someone will stay awake all night.

(2) **crám (for a test)** = push a lot of information into your mind at one time; study "at the last minute"

Note: Think of *cramming* something into a full drawer. To *cram* is to try to push something into a container (such as your brain) that is already quite full.

- I'm sorry. I can't talk to you right now. I have to go **cram for** my history midterm. Have you started studying for it yet?
- I **crammed** all night, and after the test I forgot everything!

(3) **stay úp** = not go to bed (for any reason, not just to study)

- On New Year's Eve, they **stayed up** all night. (They didn't go to bed.)
- On New Year's Eve, they **stayed up** late. (They went to bed late.)

Note: You can **stay up late *to*** study. Or, you can **stay up late *and*** study.

Your Turn

Answer these questions with a partner.

1. Have you ever **pulled an all-nighter**? If yes, when, why, and where?
2. Do you usually study *in advance*, or do you usually **cram for a test**?
3. If you need to **stay up** late to study, what do you do to stay awake?

22 Pulling an All-Nighter

2. **(júst) in the níck of tíme** = just in time; at the last possible moment

Note: When people do something in the nick of time, they feel relieved because they don't miss what they want or need to do.

Grammar Note: This expression is usually used with past tense verbs.

- We got there **(just) in the nick of time**. The movie had just started.
- You got here **in the nick of time**. We almost left without you.
- He paid his parking ticket **in the nick of time**.

ALL CLEAR?

Your Turn

Fill in the blanks with the past tense forms of these verbs: *arrive, get* (two times), *turn,* and *take.*

1. We ________ to the airport in the nick of time, so we didn't miss our flight.
2. They ________ out of the house in the nick of time—right before the fire reached their house.
3. The car ________ in the nick of time, so luckily there wasn't an accident.
4. The taxi ________ at the hospital in the nick of time, so she didn't have her baby in the back seat.
5. She ________ the chicken out of the oven in the nick of time, so luckily it didn't burn.

Think about prepositions: arrive *at* = get *to*

3. **be in hót wáter (with someone)** = be in trouble

ALL CLEAR?

A: What's wrong with her today? She looks so unhappy.
B: She's **in hot water with** her teacher because she cheated on her test.

Pulling an All-Nighter 23

- **Your Turn** sections enhance comprehension by giving students the chance to personalize and connect idioms to their own lives and experiences.

- **Grammar Practice** sections in every lesson teach students how to use idioms in complete, correct sentences.

- **Error Correction** sections provide editing practice.

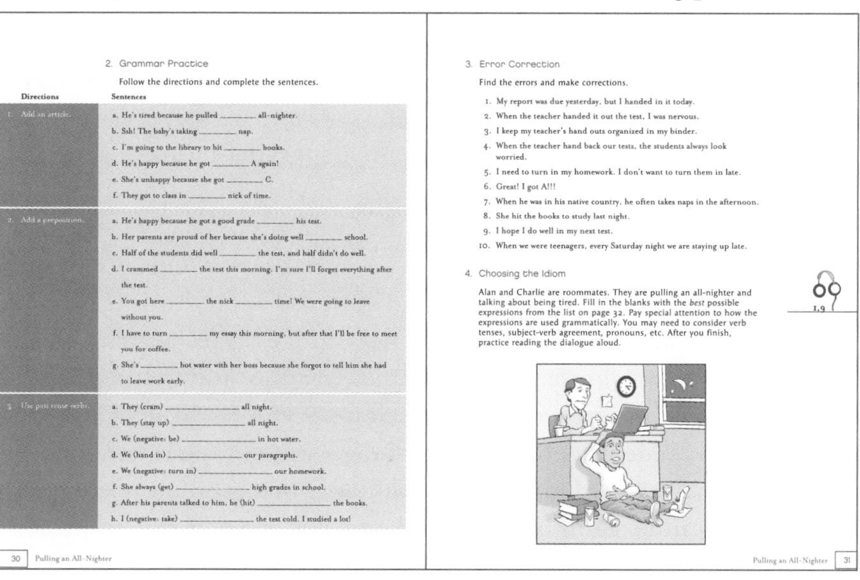

- **Culture Note** boxes in every lesson apply the theme to the outside world and encourage discussion.

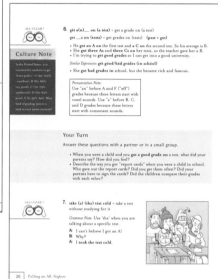

- **Communicative activities** emphasize the practical uses of idioms in everyday conversations.

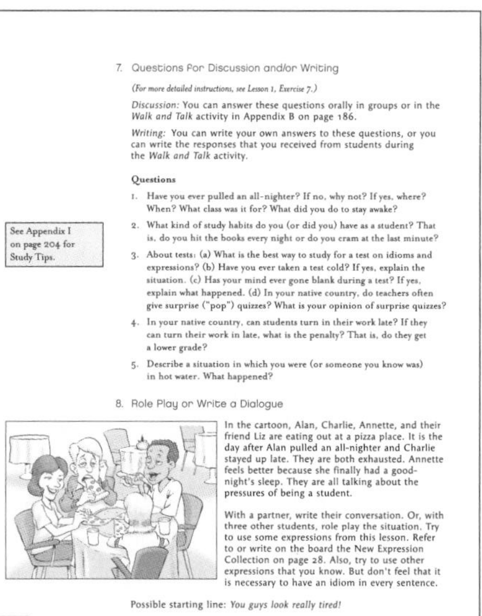

- Comprehensive **Review** sections for every lesson practice and assess key concepts.

- Opportunities for **role-playing, group work** and **delivering speeches** increase oral communication skills while meeting state standards.

All Clear 2 Listening and Speaking is the third edition of the original text in the *All Clear* series. Because the material in *All Clear 2* focuses on listening, speaking, pronunciation, culture, and public speaking in addition to idioms and expressions, this revised text would be appropriate in the following types of classes at the intermediate and high-intermediate levels: listening/speaking, idioms, vocabulary, and pronunciation.

It was in the early 1980s when I wrote the first edition of *All Clear,* which focused on idioms, and it is refreshing today to see such great interest in teaching with a lexical approach. While the initial focus of each lesson in this text is on lexical chunks of language (idioms and other expressions), students gain practice in all skill areas: listening, speaking, pronunciation, grammar, reading and writing.

It is well-known that in listening/speaking classes it can be difficult to give homework and test and grade students because of the nature of the many open-ended activities. The inclusion of idioms in these classes brings in more concrete language material that can be easily assigned as homework and subsequently assessed.

All Clear 2

- exposes students to conversational situations that can serve as a basis for conversation practice, often with a cross-cultural focus.
- provides many structured and communicative activities for speaking, listening, grammar, writing, pronunciation and public speaking practice.
- teaches students to recognize and produce high-frequency idioms and expressions.
- contextualizes the study of pronunciation by integrating it with the study of idioms.

All Clear 2 starts with an Icebreaker activity, and is then divided into eight lessons, four review sections, a pronunciation section, and eleven appendices.

Icebreaker

To get to know each other, students mill around and ask each other questions based on information taken from student questionnaires completed at the previous class meeting. A sample questionnaire and sample *Find Someone Who . . .* activity are provided.

Lessons

The lessons integrate listening, speaking, pronunciation, grammar, and writing, while focusing on teaching common expressions. Throughout each lesson, students are given opportunities to be very active and involved learners. Varied activities and numerous visuals are designed to reach students with a range of learning styles.

It is possible to move through the text in random order. Each lesson is independent, except in one area: pronunciation. If you plan to make pronunciation a substantial component of your course, you might prefer to follow the lessons in order because the pronunciation points build upon one another. The pronunciation part of each lesson appears in a separate section towards the back of the text.

You might want to start with Lesson 1, as it has more detailed instructions than the other lessons.

Warm-Up

Students answer questions about their opinions or personal experience related to the lesson theme.

Focused Listening

Before You Listen: Students look at a cartoon and try to guess what the characters are saying. NEW!

As You Listen: Students listen to a conversation with their books closed, and then answer two general questions about the main idea. They listen again as they read the conversation.

After You Listen: To check their comprehension of details, students do a *True/False* exercise. Then, by looking at paraphrases of five expressions, they try to guess meanings.

Understanding the New Expressions

This section teaches the meanings, forms, and uses of expressions that appear in the introductory conversation.

- Meanings are revealed in explanations, mini-dialogues and example sentences.
- Related expressions (those that are similar or opposite in appearance and/or meaning) are included.
- Grammar and pronunciation notes call students' attention to details about expressions. Notes about usage are also included.
- *Your Turn* activities make this section interactive. Students immediately have opportunities to work with each other and use the new expressions. NEW and INTERACTIVE!
- One *Your Turn: Listening Challenge* per lesson provides an additional listening opportunity.
- Students evaluate their understanding of expressions by indicating whether or not the meanings are *all clear.*

Exercises

Students do exercises individually, in pairs, and in groups. When students work in groups, you might want to assign roles: leader, reporter, timekeeper, participant. Group leaders should make sure that students know each other's names, that everyone participates in a balanced way, and that the group stays on task and completes the activity at hand.

The ten exercises listed below move from structured to communicative. (The exercises with an asterisk appear on the audio program.)

Focus on Form and Meaning

1. **Mini-Dialogues** (matching): In the mini-dialogues, students see the expressions in new contexts that help them understand the meanings of the expressions.*

NEW! 2. **Grammar Practice**: Given specific directions to use certain parts of speech or change verb tenses, students focus on form.

NEW! 3. **Error Correction**: Students continue to focus on form as they analyze sentences with errors.

4. **Choosing the Idiom (fill-in)**: This exercise brings together what students have worked on in the preceding three exercises—recognizing which expression to use (meaning) and providing it in the proper grammatical form.*

NEW! 5. **Sentence Writing**: In this contextualized exercise, students read stories that contain bolded paraphrases of expressions that they have studied. Then students write sentences about the story using the new expressions.

6. **Dictation**: For more listening practice, students listen to a summary of the introductory conversation using reported speech. When necessary, key words are provided to help with spelling. Dictations can be given by the teacher or a student, or the recorded program can be used. All dictations appear in Appendix A.*

Focus on Communication

7. **Questions for Discussion and/or Writing**: This communicative exercise can be done in two ways. In the first, students can ask and answer questions in small groups. In the second, students can "Walk & Talk" as they ask numerous classmates the questions. In the latter case, students can use the forms in Appendix B to take notes. Following this activity, students can write sentences with the information that they obtained from their classmates.

NEW! 8. **Role Play or Write a Dialogue**: Students role play or write a dialogue based on a cartoon.

NEW! 9. **Word Game**: Students use and supply expressions in various kinds of puzzles and games.

NEW! 10. **Public Speaking**: Public speaking activities take two forms. In one, the class asks students questions while they sit on the "Hot Seat." Suggested questions can be found in Appendix C. In the other public speaking activity, students give formal speeches on topics related to lesson themes. Suggested topics are given. Guidelines and teacher, peer, and self-evaluation forms are provided in Appendix D.

At the end of each lesson, students are encouraged to use specific strategies and techniques to help them categorize and remember new expressions. Students add expressions to the "Expression Clusters" in Appendix E and to the Expression Collections in Appendices F and G.

Review Sections

After each two lessons, a "Collocation Match-Up" exercise and a crossword puzzle provide students with opportunities for review. At the time of each review, it is suggested that students complete an evaluation of their progress using the form in Appendix H. Students might also create vocabulary cards and use other study tips described in Appendix I.

Pronunciation Section

This section, which focuses mostly on suprasegmentals (stress, intonation and rhythm), appears towards the back of the text. This allows the teacher to introduce this material if time allows and at whatever time during a lesson that may be appropriate. The contexts of the pronunciation exercises come from each lesson, providing students with meaning material for practice.

Appendices

Ten appendices provide support and supplementary material for the lessons:

A Dictations for Exercise 6
B Walk and Talk Forms for Exercise 7
C Hot Seat
D How to Make a Speech + Speech Evaluation Forms
E Expression Clusters
F Expression Collection 1—Expressions from *All Clear 2* that students hear or read outside of class
G Expression Collection 2—New expressions students hear or read outside of class
H Student Self-Evaluation Questionnaire
I Study Tips
J Guide to Pronunciation Symbols

Audio Program

The audio program uses natural speech to present the following from each lesson:

- Introductory Conversation
- Listening Challenge
- Exercise 1—Mini-Dialogues
- Exercise 4—Choosing the Idiom
- Exercise 6—Dictation
- Pronunciation

I hope that you and your students enjoy using ***All Clear 2,*** and I welcome your comments and suggestions.

Helen Kalkstein Fragiadakis
Contra Costa College
San Pablo, California

To the Student

Dear Student,

Welcome to ***All Clear 2 Listening and Speaking.*** As you use this text and improve your listening and speaking skills, you will also learn idioms and other expressions that are so necessary for effective communication in English.

Listening and Speaking

In ***All Clear 2,*** you will have many opportunities to practice and develop your listening skills. As you listen to conversations, you will listen for main points and details. You will also have the opportunity to guess the meanings of new expressions from the contexts of the conversations. In dictations and pronunciation exercises, you will have additional listening practice.

You would also no doubt like to have numerous opportunities to speak in class. Many speaking opportunities are built into this text. You will have informal conversations in pairs and small groups, and also make formal presentations to your class.

About Idioms

As all students of a foreign language know, it is important to keep adding to your knowledge of vocabulary. You probably realize that when you don't understand what you hear, it is not always because someone is speaking too fast. It is often because you don't know some of the words or expressions being used.

As you work on increasing your vocabulary, it is best to not focus only on individual words because so much vocabulary comes in word groups—in phrases and expressions. Words that naturally go together are called *collocations.* When you learn more and more of these groups of words, you will find that your confidence will increase and that you will have the courage to use English more often.

In ***All Clear 2,*** the springboards for listening and discussion come from introductory conversations that contain numerous phrases and expressions. Some of these phrases and expressions are "idiomatic" and have special meanings. An example of an idiomatic expression is *to get cold feet,* which means to become so nervous about starting something new (a life change such as a marriage or a new job) *that you think you shouldn't do it.* Your feet are not cold!

I've taught students at your level for many years, and have found that the following is what they need and want when studying idioms:

- to recognize and use the most common expressions
- to see numerous examples of the expressions in different contexts and in natural language
- to clarify how these expressions resemble or are different from other expressions they've heard
- to learn how to pronounce these expressions, not only alone, but also as parts of sentences
- to know the grammar associated with each expression
- to know any particular information about the use of expressions—for example, whether an expression is appropriate to say to a boss or a teacher as well as to a best friend
- to have a lot of opportunities to practice using the expressions in both speaking and writing

If you want to improve your listening and pronunciation skills, have meaningful discussions on topics that interest you, increase your vocabulary, and in general increase your confidence in your ability to use English, then our goals are the same.

Good luck to you, and I hope that you find the material in this text to be enjoyable and *all clear.*

Sincerely,

Helen Kalkstein Fragiadakis

Helen Kalkstein Fragiadakis

Directions

1. At the first class meeting, the students (and maybe also the teacher) should fill out the questionnaire below (or an adapted form).
2. At the second class, the students *Walk and Talk,* using the form on the next page. The items they ask are their responses taken from the questionnaires that they filled out at the first class meeting.

STUDENT QUESTIONNAIRE

What is your name? (Last)_________________ (First) _________________

What name do you want everyone to call you in class? _________________

Where are you from? _________________

What is your native language? _________________

How long have you been in this English-speaking country? _________________

OR

Have you ever been in a country where English is the main language?

__Yes __No

If yes, where? _________________

What language or languages do you speak at home? _________________

Do you work? _________________

If yes, what do you do? _________________

Are you a high school or college student? __Yes __No

If yes, what are you studying? _________________

What do you like to do in your free time?

What is something interesting about you or someone in your family?

What do you want to learn in this class?

Is there anything that you would like to add? If yes, please write it here.

Walk and Talk

Stand up, get out of your seat, and get to know your classmates. Find out the information in this Walk and Talk activity by talking to at least five different students. The questions you ask are based on the student questionnaires that you previously completed.

Steps

- Get up and ask a student the first question.
  If the student says "Yes," then ask "What's your (first) name?" If necessary, also ask "How do you spell that?" Then write the student's first name on the line at the right. If a student says "No," say "Thanks anyway" and move on to another student.
- Continue until you have a name next to each question.
- After everyone is finished, your teacher can ask for the names of students who said 'Yes' to each question and ask them for more information.

SAMPLE

Find someone who . . .	**First Name**
1. is from Mexico (Are you from Mexico?)	__________
2. speaks three languages (Do you speak three languages?)	__________
3. speaks a little bit of English at home (Do you speak a little bit of English at home?)	__________
4. is a cook/manicurist/doctor/businessman/businesswoman (Are you a doctor?)	__________
5. plays the guitar (Do you play the guitar?)	__________
6. has four sisters and five brothers (Do you have four sisters and five brothers?)	__________
7. speaks Japanese (Do you speak Japanese?)	__________
8. plans to get a degree in engineering (Do you plan to get a degree in engineering?)	__________

Lesson 1

Getting Cold Feet

Theme: Getting Married

Warm-Up

1. If you are married, were you very nervous before your wedding? If yes, what were you worried about?
2. Think about a time in your life when you were planning to do something, but then got very scared and didn't do it. What happened?

   Possible situations:

   - a job interview
   - a scary or dangerous kind of sport
   - a place where you didn't know anyone
   - a situation in which you were going to tell someone something serious, but you changed your mind

Focused Listening

Before You Listen

Rick and Jana are going to get married. What do you think Rick and Tim in the cartoon are saying to each other? What do you think Jana and Ellen are saying?

As You Listen

(A) Close your book. Listen to the conversations between Jana and Ellen, and Rick and Tim to find the answers to these questions.

How does Jana feel? How does Rick feel?

(B) Listen again, but this time read the conversation as you listen.

ELLEN: Can you believe it Jana? Your wedding is in two weeks!

JANA: I know.

ELLEN: What's wrong?

JANA: Well . . . I think I'**m getting cold feet**.

ELLEN: Oh, don't worry. That's normal. That's how I felt before I married Tim. But everything will be fine. You and Rick are really great together.

JANA: I know, but maybe we should wait. We **can't** even **afford to** buy furniture!

ELLEN: Oh, so it's money that's making you **have second thoughts**. But **deep down** you really want to get married.

JANA: You're right. I really do. I'**m dying to** marry Rick.

* * * * *

TIM: Hey, Rick. What's wrong?

RICK: I don't know. I just hope I'm ready to get married.

TIM: Uh-oh! **Are** you **getting cold feet**?

RICK: I guess you could say that. I'**m about to** change my life **for good,** so I'**m kind of** nervous.

TIM: OK. Then **call off** the wedding.

RICK: But I'**m dying to** marry Jana!

TIM: And she'**s dying to** marry you. So why don't you just take a deep breath and **calm down**!?

After You Listen

(A) Read the sentences about the conversations. Circle *T* for *true*, *F* for *false*, or *?* if you don't know.

1. Rick and Jana are going to get married in two weeks. T F ?
2. Jana is nervous about getting married, but Rick isn't nervous. T F ?
3. Ellen and Tim are married. T F ?
4. Ellen thinks Rick and Jana should get married after they have enough money for furniture. T F ?
5. Rick and Jana will have a happy marriage. T F ?

(B) **Guess the Meanings**
When you say the same thing with different words, you are paraphrasing. Read the paraphrases below, and find an expression in the conversations that means the same thing. Make sure the paraphrase would easily fit into the conversations.

Paraphrase	Idiomatic Expression
Example: *getting very, very nervous*	getting cold feet
1. don't have enough money to	__________
2. really want to	__________
3. relax	__________
4. in your heart	__________
5. forever	__________

(C) Say the conversations in groups of four. Then, have four students say the conversations in front of the class.

Understanding the New Expressions

Work with Others

If you're working with a partner or in a small group, read the short dialogues and examples for each expression aloud. Also, complete the Your Turn exercises together. For each expression, circle *Yes* or *No* to show if you understand. If you circled *No,* highlight or underline what is unclear, and ask questions for clarification.

Figure It out on Your Own

Read the short dialogues and examples for each expression. Also, complete the Your Turn exercises that don't need partners. Then, for each expression, circle *Yes* or *No* to show if you understand. If you circled *No,* highlight or underline what is still unclear, and ask questions in class for clarification.

1. **gét cóld féet (and)(about)** = become so nervous about starting something new (a life change such as a marriage or a new job) *that you think you shouldn't do it*

   háve cóld féet (and) (about) = be so nervous about starting something new *that you think you shouldn't do it*

   (past: got cold feet = had cold feet)

Notes:

- *To get cold feet* and *to be nervous* are not exactly the same. When you have cold feet, you are thinking about *not* doing something that you are afraid of. For example, if you are very afraid of a test and go home, you *have cold feet.* But if you are afraid of a test and still take it, you *are nervous.*
- There are two possible results after getting cold feet: (a) the person decides to take a big step and do something, *OR* (b) he or she decides *not* to do something.

A: Did they get married?
B: Yes. Two weeks before the wedding, she started to **get cold feet.** But then she relaxed and was fine.

A: Did they get married?
B: No. At the last minute, she **got cold feet and** canceled the wedding.

Grammar Note: "About" is a preposition, and it is necessary to have a noun after a preposition. If you want to use a verb after *get/have cold feet about,* you need to change the verb into a noun form called a "gerund." To do this, add *-ing* to the verb. Examples: get cold feet about *buying, going, doing, leaving, getting,* etc.

- I hope you won't **get cold feet *about*** the trip.
- When she heard about the low salary, she **got cold feet *about* taking** the job.
- He **had cold feet *about* hiking** so far in the mountains, so he decided to just take a short day hike.

Your Turn

Did you ever get cold feet? Complete the chart. Then, talk about your "yes" answers with a partner. Say, "I got cold feet when . . ."

Situation	**Did you get cold feet? (Yes or No)**	**If you got cold feet, explain what happened.**
1. getting married	____________	____________
2. starting a new job	____________	____________
3. performing in front of an audience (acting, singing, playing an instrument)	____________	____________
4. making a speech	____________	____________
5. playing on a sports team	____________	____________
6. coming to this country (if it's not your native country)	____________	____________
7. Other: ____________	____________	____________

2. **can/cán't/could/cóuldn't affórd** = have or not have enough money
can't afford *to do* (verb) *something*
can't afford *something* (noun)

A: I didn't know you have a job.
B: Well, I **can't afford** to go to school full-time. So I work and go to school part-time.

A: I thought you were going to buy a new car.
B: I wanted to, but I **couldn't afford** one. I had to get a used car, but it's OK.

A: That camera is so expensive!
B: Don't worry. I **can afford** it.

Your Turn

Complete the sentences with a partner. Use phrases with *afford* in 3 and 4.

1. They can afford to ________________, but they can't afford to ________________.
2. They can afford a(n) ________________, but they can't afford a(n) ________________.
3. Last year he ________________ a new car, but now he can.
4. Last year he ________________ a long vacation, but this year he can't.

3. **háve/hád sécond thóughts** = think that a decision that you made before might not be a good one; have doubts about something

have second thoughts about *something* or *someone*
("Thoughts" is a noun, not the past of the verb *think.*)
have second thoughts about *doING something*

Grammar Note: Remember that "about" is a preposition, and it is necessary to have a noun after a preposition. If you want to use a verb after *have second thoughts about,* you need to change the verb into a "gerund." To do this, add *-ing* to the verb. Examples: have second thoughts about *buying, going, doing, leaving, getting,* etc.

A: They'**re having second thoughts about** that house.
B: What do you mean?
A: Well, it's an old house and they're afraid that they'll have a lot of problems if they live there.

A: What do you think of the new guy?
B: I'm afraid I'**m having second thoughts about** him. At first, I was sure he was right for the job, but now I'm not so sure. His work isn't as good as I expected.

A: I need to talk to you. I'**m having second thoughts about buying** that car.
B: What's the problem?
A: Well, first of all, it's really expensive. And second of all, it's an automatic, and I want a manual transmission.

Your Turn

Complete the sentences with a partner. Use gerunds (verbs + ING).

1. They had second thoughts about (get) ________________ married.
2. Did you have second thoughts about (take) ________________ this class?
3. She's having second thoughts about (quit) ________________ her job.
4. I'm having second thoughts about (go) ________________ to the beach today.

4. **déep dówn** = deep in your heart—your true feelings such as anger, love, or happiness

Grammar Note: It is not correct to say "I deep down want to go home." It is correct to say, "Deep down, I want to go home."

A: I told them that I wanted to fly, but **deep down** I'd really like to drive.
B: Why?
A: I've never told anyone this before, but I'm afraid of flying.

A: Look at how the politicians are all smiling at each other. But **deep down** they really don't like each other.
B: How do you know?

Your Turn

Talk to two classmates. Write short notes in the chart. Then, write four sentences about your classmates with the expression *deep down.*

Questions	Classmate 1	Classmate 2
1. Deep down, where would you really like to be right now?		
2. Deep down, do you really want to study English, or are you studying it because it's a requirement?		

5. **be dýing to (dó something)** = want to do something very, very much

A: That new movie is finally here. I'**m dying to** see it. Want to come?
B: Maybe. What's it about?

A: Why are you going home so early?
B: I'**m dying to** get the mail. I'm expecting something special.

Similar Expressions:

be dýing of thírst = be very, very thirsty
be dýing of húnger = be very, very hungry

- It's so hot and I'**m dying of thirst**. Let's stop and get a drink.
- I haven't eaten since this morning and I'**m dying of hunger**.

Your Turn: Listening Challenge

First, listen to only Part A of the conversation. Then, with a partner, come up with possibilities about what the woman is dying to do. To find out, listen to Part B.

We think she's dying to ______________________________.

6. **be (júst) about (réady) to (dó something)** = be almost ready to (do something)

- TIM: Hi, Rick! I **was (just) about to** call you.

A: Hello.
B: Hi, Jana.
A: Oh, hi Ellen. How are you today?
B: Pretty good. I wanted to know how you're feeling.
A: Thanks for asking. I'm much better. But listen, I have my keys in my hand. I'**m about ready to** leave because my class starts in 20 minutes. Can I call you back later?

7. **for góod** = forever, permanently

Note: Use this expression when you are talking about things that can or can't be permanent (relationships such as marriage, smoking, where you live, etc.). It is not correct to say that you are "studying for good."

A: I'm giving up smoking **for good**. I promise.
B: I'm so glad to hear that!

A: I just got a letter from my son—finally.
B: Any news?
A: Yeah—big news. He's coming home **for good**. You know—he's been traveling for over two years.
B: That long? Well then he probably really wants to come home by now.

8. **be kínd of = be sórt of** = to some degree/somewhere in the middle

Note: We often use these expressions to soften a statement about how we feel about ourselves or something else. This way we sound less direct and more polite. Instead of saying "I'm hungry," people often say "I'm *kind of* hungry." If food is too spicy, it sounds softer to say, "It's *kind of* spicy."

Grammar Note: Use an adjective after these expressions.

Pronunciation Note: "Kind of" sounds like "kinda." "Sort of" sounds like "sorda."

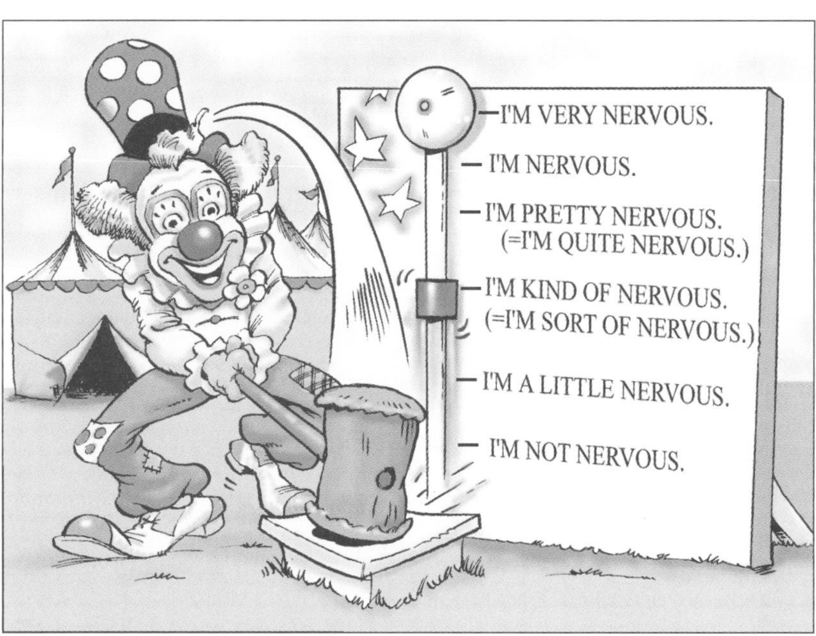

A: Do you want to take a walk?
B: I'm sorry. Not right now. I'**m kind of** tired.

A: How's the chicken?
B: Well, it'**s sort of** spicy.
A: You don't like it?

9. **call (something) óff** = cancel an event (a meeting, a party, a sports event, etc.)

Grammar Note: **Call off** is a verb with two parts. It is called a *phrasal verb.*

- When you use a noun with this expression, you can put the noun *after* the two words or *between* them.

A: What are you doing home?
B: They **called off** the game because it started to rain.
OR
They **called** the game **off** because it started to rain.

- When you use a pronoun with this expression, put the pronoun *between* the two words. It is not correct to put a pronoun after a phrasal verb.

A: Isn't there a game today?
B: No. They **called it off** because of the rain.
(NOT: They ~~called off it~~.) (**it** = game)

10. **calm (someone) dówn** = relax

A: Hello.
B: Martha? I need to talk to you. I'm so worried. I don't know what to do.
A: **Calm down** Angela. Take a deep breath. Tell me what's wrong. Don't worry. I'll help you.

A: Did you talk to Angela?
B: Yes, she called. I **calmed her down.**

Your Turn

Answer these questions with a partner or in a small group.

1. When you are upset about something, what is the best way for you to calm down?
2. When you are talking to someone who is upset, what can you do and what can you say to help him or her calm down?

NEW EXPRESSION COLLECTION		
get/have cold feet	be dying to do something	call off
can/can't afford	be just about ready to do something	calm down
have second thoughts	for good	
deep down	be kind of/be sort of	

Exercises

(See page 157 for pronunciation exercises for Lesson 1. Focus: Sentence Stress.)

1. Mini-Dialogues

Read the sentences in Column A. Choose the *best* response from Column B. Not all responses can be used.

When checking this exercise in class, perform each mini-dialogue. One student should read an item from Column A, and another student should read the response from Column B.

1A

___ **1.** He has two cars and a boat—and he works in a fast-food restaurant!

___ **2.** Dad, I'm dying of thirst.

___ **3.** I thought you were going to make a speech in front of all the teachers.

___ **4.** What are you doing here? I thought you were on a trip.

___ **5.** All right. I'll go with you.

1B

a. Well, go get yourself a glass of water!

b. No, I'll get someone else to come with me. I know that deep down you really just want to stay home.

c. It's kind of difficult.

d. How can he afford those things?

e. I didn't go because I had second thoughts about spending all that money.

f. I was, but I got cold feet.

2A

___ **1.** I'm not staying here for good. I want to see the world.

___ **2.** I'm dying to meet her. Can you introduce us?

___ **3.** We were just about to go to bed when the earthquake hit.

___ **4.** I heard they canceled the party.

___ **5.** The kids are really excited. Can you calm them down?

2B

a. That's right. And I was sort of happy that they called it off because I didn't really want to go.

b. Do your parents know what you want to do?

c. What did you do?

d. What should I do?

e. You couldn't afford to go.

f. Well, I don't know. She already has a boyfriend.

2. Grammar Practice

Follow the directions and complete the sentences.

Directions	Sentences
1. Add an irregular past tense verb.	a. When they were younger, they (negative) ________________ afford to buy a house. b. She ________________ second thoughts about that job, so she didn't take it. c. When he got to the job interview, he ________________ cold feet and turned around and went right back home! d. We ________________ dying to see that show, but we couldn't get tickets. e. They ________________ just about ready to have dinner when the doorbell rang.
2. Add a gerund.	a. Their trip is next week, but now they're having second thoughts about ________________. b. He registered for five classes, but now he's having second thoughts about (take) ________________ all of them. c. We were planning to move, but now we're having second thoughts about ________________ in the mountains. d. At first, he had cold feet about (take) ________________ the job, but when he heard about the high salary, he accepted it.
3. Add an infinitive (*to* + verb) and complete each sentence.	a. You can afford ________________ that car. b. I can't afford ________________. c. I'm dying ________________. d. They were just about ready ________________ when the phone rang.
4. Add a preposition.	a. I'm kind ________________ tired. I think I'll stay home. b. The kids are dying ________________ thirst. Let's get them some water. c. We're having second thoughts ________________ getting that computer. d. They said they're going to stay here ________________ good. e. We got cold feet ________________ buying that house because it was so expensive. f. They called ________________ the game because of the bad weather.

3. Error Correction

Find the errors and make corrections.

1. We didn't drive to New York because we get cold feet.
2. We had cold feet about drive there.
3. He can't afford an expensive present, so he bought her flowers.
4. Can you afford live in San Francisco?
5. It's raining. I'm having second thoughts about go out tonight.
6. I'm dying for have an ice cream cone.
7. English is kind hard.
8. We can't go to the party. They called off it.
9. He read the kids a story to calm him down.
10. I'm dying thirst. Do you know where I can buy a bottle of water?

4. Choosing the Idiom

Rick and Jana are getting married today, and Tim and Rick are talking before the ceremony. Fill in the blanks with the *best* possible expressions from the list. Pay special attention to how the expressions are used grammatically. You may need to consider verb tenses, subject-verb agreement, pronouns, etc. After you finish, practice reading the dialogue aloud.

be about to	be dying to
calm down	(negative) have second thoughts
cold feet	kind of

TIM: Still have (1) ______________________ ?

RICK: No. And I (2) ______________________ either. I feel great.

TIM: I can see that. You look really happy. So does Jana.

RICK: Where is she? Did you see her?

TIM: Oh, yeah. But *you* can't till the ceremony.

till = until

RICK: That's a crazy superstition. Show me where she is. I (3) ______________ ______________ see her.

TIM: Oh, no. Her mother would be really mad. She believes it's bad luck if the bride and groom see each other before the ceremony.

RICK: Did she really say that? I can't believe it! Hey—you have the rings, don't you?

TIM: The rings? Uh-oh! I think I left them at home. I (4) ______________ ______________ put them in my pocket when my phone rang . . .

RICK: You forgot the rings?

TIM: (5) ______________________ Rick! I was just kidding. I have them.

RICK: This is no time for joking. I'm (6) ______________________ nervous, you know.

TIM: *Kind of* nervous? Hah! I've never seen you so nervous. Why don't you come over here and sit down?

Culture Note

Some people believe that it is bad luck for a bride and groom to see each other before their wedding ceremony. Do you have the same superstition in your native country?

5. Sentence Writing

Read the paragraphs. Then, write sentences about Nancy and her job. In each sentence, use at least one expression from the box. (**Bolded** words and phrases in the story represent where expressions can go.) Underline the expressions that you use.

Remember to pay attention to grammar details: verb tenses, prepositions, articles, singular and plural nouns, etc.

Hi! I'm Nancy. I really need your advice, so I hope you'll listen to my story. I've been at the same job for about eight years now, and **I really really want to** leave because it's getting **kind of** boring. Anyway, I had some job interviews recently and I think they liked me at the last one. But now **I'm not sure I want to change jobs**. I'm so comfortable where I am and sometimes I think I should stay there **forever**. I tell you, I'm so nervous about making a change—if they call me right now, I think I'll have to say no.

But the good thing about the possible new job is that the salary is higher. More money would be nice. Right now, **I don't have enough money to** buy a car and I really need one because my old one has so many miles on it.

Please tell me what to do. **I** just can't **relax**, but I need to. Yesterday, when I **was at my door and ready to** go out, the phone rang and I jumped and my heart beat so fast that I thought I'd explode! I was sure it was about that job, but it was my mother. I can't live this way!

can/can't afford	be dying to	calm down	for good
be just about ready to	sort of	have second thoughts about	

Example: *Nancy* ***is dying to*** *leave her job.*

6. Dictation

Your teacher or one of your classmates will read the dictation for this lesson from Appendix A, or you will listen to the recorded dictation. You will hear the dictation three times. First, just listen. Second, as you listen, write the dictation on a separate piece of paper. Skip lines. Third, listen again and check what you have written. Then, look at the dictation in Appendix A on page 183.

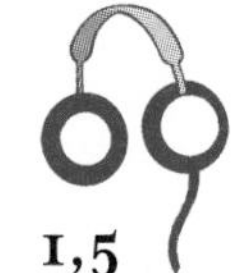

Key Words: swimming pool, furniture, shouldn't, wedding, clearly

7. Questions for Discussion and/or Writing

Discussion: Choose *one* of the activities below.

- Walk around your classroom and ask various classmates discussion questions. Take short notes. Forms for this *Walk and Talk* activity appear in Appendix B on page 185.
- In groups of three or four, answer the discussion questions that follow. Assign a discussion leader. The leader should make sure that everyone participates.

Writing: Choose *one* of the activities below.

- If you have done the *Walk and Talk* activity, write the responses of the students you talked to. Give their names and include the expressions that appear in the questions. To be sure that your sentences contain the correct information, you can *Walk and Talk* again and show your writing to the students who supplied the information.
- Write your own answers to the questions below. In numbers 1, 3, and 4 be sure to include the expressions in your sentences.

Questions

1. Did you ever get cold feet before a big event? If yes, what happened—did you change your plans, or did you deal with the scary situation?
2. As you can see from the conversation in Exercise 4, some American people have superstitions about getting married. Do you have superstitions related to wedding customs in your native country? What are they?
3. Deep down, do you *really* want to learn English, or are you studying it because (a) your school requires it, (b) your parents want you to learn it, or (c) it is necessary for your work? Explain your answer.
4. What is something that you are dying to do within the next five years? Why?

8. Role Play or Write a Dialogue

In the cartoon, two friends are having a very serious conversation. One of the friends is having second thoughts about a big change in his or her life—getting married, moving to a new city or country, or starting a new job. The other friend is giving advice.

With a partner, role play or write the conversation between the friends. Try to use some expressions from this lesson. Refer to or write on the board the New Expression Collection on page 10. Also, try to use other expressions that you know. But don't feel that it is necessary to have an idiom in every sentence.

Possible starting line: *What's wrong? You look upset.*

9. Unscramble and Find the Secret Message

Unscramble the words to make sentences with the expressions from this lesson. Then, find the secret message at the bottom of the page.

EH IDDN'T TGE CDOL EEFT EBEORF SIH GWDDNIE

YTHE'RE NAISGYT ERTHE RFO GODO

CLMA NDWO! I'LL LALC FOF EHT GWDIDEN

DEPE WDON, TYHE ODN'T TNAW TO OG

I SAW SUTJ TBUOA YDEAR OT AYS "YES," BTU I DDIN'T

NAER'T YOU IYNDG TO KETA A BAKRE

I'M IYNGD FO THTRSI

EW CAN'T AFRODF THE PTIR

I VHAE ON DNOCES HOTGSTUH

TI WSA INDK OF A DRHA CNSIOIDE

SHTI ZELZUP IS ROTS FO UFN

Secret Message:

10. Public Speaking

Sit on the Hot Seat

Interview a classmate. Choose one student to come to the "Hot Seat" (a chair) in the front of the classroom. Or, get into groups and choose one student in each group to be on the "Hot Seat." This student will answer questions. See Appendix C on page 193 for sample questions. It is best to *not* ask personal questions.

Make a Speech

Prepare a five minute speech on one of the following topics. See Appendix D on page 194 for more information.

- Dating and engagement customs in my native country
- A typical wedding in my native country
- Male and female roles in my native country
- Five idioms with the word "heart"

Note: Search the Internet if you need to get extra information.

Keep an Inventory

Add to:

Expression Clusters—Appendix E

Expression Collections—Appendices F and G

Lesson 2

Pulling an All-Nighter

Theme: Students Under Pressure

Warm-Up

1. In your native country, is it common for students to stay up all night studying? If yes, when does this happen? What do they do to stay awake?
2. Did you ever have to give work to a teacher late because you forgot to do it or because something happened? If yes, what did you do and what did your teacher say?

Focused Listening

Before You Listen

Alan and Annette in the cartoon are walking together on a college campus. What do you think they are talking about?

As You Listen

Ⓐ Close your book. Listen to the conversations between Alan and Annette to find the answers to these questions.

How does Annette feel? Why? Is Alan helpful?

Ⓑ Listen again, but this time read the conversations as you listen.

psych = psychology

ALAN: Annette, is everything OK? You look really tired.

ANNETTE: It's that obvious? Well, you're right. I *am* tired. Last night I **pulled an all-nighter** writing a paper for my psych class.

ALAN: Did you finish it?

ANNETTE: Yeah, and just **in the nick of time**. I e-mailed it to my professor five minutes before the deadline.

ALAN: Well, that was close. Are you going home now?

ANNETTE: No—I have to hurry to my history class. See you later.

* * * * *

(A few hours later)

ANNETTE: Alan—**I'm** really **in hot water**. My history teacher gave us a surprise quiz and I couldn't remember anything. **My mind went totally blank**. I didn't even want to **hand in** my quiz because I knew everything was wrong. Oh, I can't believe this! I'm going to **get an F on** a test!

ALAN: That happened to me once, but it wasn't a surprise quiz. I just got the date of the test wrong, so I didn't study. I **took the test cold** and **didn't do well**.

ANNETTE: What grade did you get?

ALAN: I think I got a C.

ANNETTE: Well, at least a C is passing. I'm going to get an F!

ALAN: Listen Annette, you need to take it easy. For all you know, you passed the quiz. So why don't you go home and **take a nap**?

ANNETTE: That's a good idea, but I have another class at 2:00, and we're going to have a test. I need to go to the library to **hit the books**.

ALAN: What a day you're having!

ANNETTE: **You can say *that* again!**

After You Listen

Ⓐ Read the sentences about the conversations. Circle *T* for *true*, *F* for *false*, or *?* if you don't know.

1.	Annette has a lot to do.	T	F	?
2.	Alan has a lot to do.	T	F	?
3.	Alan is Annette's boyfriend.	T	F	?
4.	Annette gave her paper to her psychology teacher late.	T	F	?
5.	Annette is going to get an F on her history quiz.	T	F	?

Ⓑ **Guess the Meanings**

Below is a list of paraphrases of five of the idiomatic expressions in the conversation. On your own or with a partner, try to guess the five. To do this, make sure that what is written below would easily fit in the conversation.

Paraphrase	Idiomatic Expression
Example: *be in trouble*	be in hot water
1. study	______________
2. give (submit)	______________
3. stayed up all night	______________
4. sleep for a short time	______________
5. right (immediately) before the deadline (the last minute)	______________

Ⓒ Say the conversations in pairs. Then have two students say the conversations in front of the class.

Understanding the New Expressions

Work with Others

If you're working with a partner or in a small group, read the short dialogues and examples for each expression aloud. Also, complete the Your Turn exercises together. For each expression, circle *Yes* or *No* to show if you understand. If you circled *No,* highlight or underline what is unclear, and ask questions for clarification.

Figure It out on Your Own

Read the short dialogues and examples for each expression. Also, complete the Your Turn exercises that don't need partners. Then, for each expression, circle *Yes* or *No* to show if you understand. If you circled *No,* highlight or underline what is still unclear, and ask questions in class for clarification.

ALL CLEAR ?
Yes No

1. **púll an all-níghter** = stay awake all night to study

A: I can't believe the test is next week! There's so much to study!

B: I know. Maybe we should start studying together right now. I don't want to **pull an all-nighter** again the night before the test. The last time I did that, I was really tired and got a terrible grade.

Similar Expressions:

(1) **búrn the mídnight óil** = stay up very late working or studying

Note: This is an old-fashioned expression that is not very common today, but you may hear it. It comes from the time when people used oil lamps for light. It does not necessarily mean that someone will stay awake all night.

(2) **crám (for a test)** = push a lot of information into your mind at one time; study "at the last minute"

Note: Think of *cramming* something into a full drawer. To *cram* is to try to push something into a container (such as your brain) that is already quite full.

- I'm sorry. I can't talk to you right now. I have to go **cram for** my history midterm. Have you started studying for it yet?
- I **crammed** all night, and after the test I forgot everything!

(3) **stay úp** = not go to bed (for any reason, not just to study)

- On New Year's Eve, they **stayed up** all night. (They didn't go to bed.)
- On New Year's Eve, they **stayed up** late. (They went to bed late.)

Note: You can **stay up late *to*** study. Or, you can **stay up late *and*** study.

Your Turn

Answer these questions with a partner.

1. Have you ever **pulled an all-nighter**? If yes, when, why, and where?
2. Do you usually study *in advance,* or do you usually **cram for a test**?
3. If you need to **stay up** late to study, what do you do to stay awake?

2. **(júst) in the níck of tíme** = just in time; at the last possible moment

Note: When people do something in the nick of time, they feel relieved because they don't miss what they want or need to do.

Grammar Note: This expression is usually used with past tense verbs.

- We got there **(just) in the nick of time.** The movie had just started.
- You got here **in the nick of time.** We almost left without you.
- He paid his parking ticket **in the nick of time.**

Your Turn

Fill in the blanks with the past tense forms of these verbs: *arrive, get* (two times), *turn,* and *take.*

1. We ________________ to the airport in the nick of time, so we didn't miss our flight.
2. They ________________ out of the house in the nick of time—right before the fire reached their house.
3. The car ________________ in the nick of time, so luckily there wasn't an accident.
4. The taxi ________________ at the hospital in the nick of time, so she didn't have her baby in the back seat.
5. She ________________ the chicken out of the oven in the nick of time, so luckily it didn't burn.

Think about prepositions:
arrive *at* = get *to*

3. **be in hót wáter (with someone)** = be in trouble

A: What's wrong with her today? She looks so unhappy.

B: She's **in hot water with** her teacher because she cheated on her test.

Your Turn: Listening Challenge

Listen to the recording to find out why the speaker is in hot water.

He's in hot water because ______________________________.

ALL CLEAR ?

4. **my mínd wént (tótally) blánk** = I couldn't remember anything

Note:

A "blank" is an empty space. If your mind "goes blank," your mind suddenly (and temporarily) feels empty.

- At first, when I looked at the test, **my mind went blank**. So, to calm down, I closed my eyes for a minute or two. Then everything came back to me. I think I got an A!

ALL CLEAR ?

Yes No

5. **hand ín (something) = turn ín (something)** = submit; give work to a teacher

Note:

When you submit work in person (face to face), you *hand it in* or *turn it in.* But when you submit your work by mail or e-mail, you *turn it in.* Use "hand in" only when you are giving the work directly to someone.

A: I'm so busy. I don't know what to do first.
B: What do you have to do?
A: I have to **turn in** two papers by next Tuesday.
B: I know how you feel. I just **handed** two **in** last week.

Grammar Note:

Hand in and **turn in** are verbs with two parts. They are *phrasal verbs.*

- When you use a noun with these expressions, you can put the noun *after* the two words or *between* them.

They **handed in** their tests.	They **handed** their tests **in.**
They **turned in** their tests.	They **turned** their tests **in.**

- When you use a pronoun with this expression, put the pronoun *between* the two words. It is not correct to put a pronoun after a phrasal verb.

They **handed** *them* **in.**	~~They handed in them~~.
They **turned** *it* **in.**	~~They turned in it~~.

Similar expressions with 'hand' (these are used in school situations):

(1) **hand báck** = return, give back student papers that had been turned in (verb)

STUDENT: When **will** you **hand back** our tests?

TEACHER: I'**ll hand** them **back** in a few days.

Note: Teachers **hand** tests and other material **back TO** students:

TEACHER: I'**m going to hand back** your tests **to** you at the end of class.

(2) **hand óut** = give out; a teacher or helper hands out papers to a class (verb)

TEACHER: Please clear your desks. I'm ready to **hand** the quizzes **out**.

(*OR:* I'm ready to **hand out** the quizzes.)

(3) **hándout(s)** = lesson material on a sheet of paper that a teacher gives to each student (noun)

- STUDENT: I was absent yesterday. Can I please have the **handout**?
- STUDENT: We don't have a book in that class. We use lots of **handouts**.

Your Turn

Complete these sentences with a partner. Use forms of *hand in, turn in, hand back, hand out,* and *handout.* Pay attention to verb tenses.

Teachers	hand things out hand things back give handouts
Students	hand things in turn things in get handouts

1. I didn't write my paragraph last night, so I need to write it now. My teacher wants me to ______________ by 2:00.
2. I know that we have to do three grammar exercises for homework. But I don't know if our teacher wants us to ______________.
3. Tests always make me nervous. On the day of a test, when my teacher ______________ tests, my hands get cold.
4. After I take tests, I always worry about my grade. When my teacher ______________ tests that she has corrected, my stomach hurts.
5. I studied my textbook and the ______________ for the quiz.
6. Last week, when my teacher ______________ our tests and I saw that I got an A, I was really surprised.
7. I was absent yesterday. Can I make a copy of your ______________?
8. Yesterday, when I ______________ my homework late, my teacher told me that next time, she won't accept any more late work.

ALL CLEAR ?

Yes No

Culture Note

In the United States, it is common for students to get 'letter grades'—A (90-100%—excellent), B (80-89%-very good), C (70-79%-satisfactory), D (60-69%-poor), F (0-59%-fail). What kind of grading system is used in your native country?

6. **gét a(n)___ on (a tést)** = get a grade on (a test)

get ___s on (tests) = get grades on (tests) **(past = got)**

- He **got an A on** the first test and **a C on** the second test. So his average is B.
- She **got three As** and **three Cs on** her tests, so the teacher gave her a B.
- I'm trying to **get good grades** so I can get into a good university.

Similar Expression: **gét góod/bád grádes (in schóol)**

- She **got bad grades in** school, but she became rich and famous.

> *Pronunciation Note:*
> Use "an" before A and F ("eff") grades because these letters start with vowel sounds. Use "a" before B, C, and D grades because these letters start with consonant sounds.

Your Turn

Answer these questions with a partner or in a small group.

- When you were a child and you **got a good grade on** a test, what did your parents say? How did you feel?
- Describe the way you got "report cards" when you were a child in school. Who gave out the report cards? Did you get them often? Did your parents have to sign the cards? Did the children compare their grades with each other?

ALL CLEAR ?

7. **táke (a) (the) tést cóld** = take a test without studying for it

Grammar Note: Use 'the' when you are talking about a specific test.

A: I can't believe I got an A!
B: Why?
A: I **took the test cold**.

8. **(not) dó wéll on (a tést)** = (not) get a good grade on a test

- I want to **do well on** this test so I can keep my A average.
- He **didn't do well on** the last test so the teacher wants to talk to him.

Similar Expressions:

(1) **(not) do well *in* (a class)/*in* school**

- Last semester **I did well in** history, but I **didn't do well in** biology.
- Her parents want to talk to the teacher because she **isn't doing well in school.**

(2) **How did you do (on the test)?**

Note:
This is a personal question that someone can ask after a test. Use responses from the column on the right if you don't want to give a specific answer.

Before you know your test grade: How did you do on the test?	I don't know./I'm not sure./I think I did OK.
After you get your grade: How did you do on the test?	I did OK.

Note:
Don't confuse this question with *How do you do?*

How do you do? is a response that people use when they are introduced to someone and want to be formal. It is not a true question:

KATE: Anne, I'd like to introduce you to Jim Brown. Jim, this is Anne Carroll.

ANNE: **How do you do?**

JIM: Nice to meet you.

9. **táke a náp/táke náps** = sleep for a short time

A: What time is it?
B: About 2:00, I think. Why?
A: I think I'**ll take a nap** for a half hour or so. I'm really tired.

- The baby **takes** two **naps** a day.
- I have a lot of energy right now because I **took a nap**.

ALL CLEAR ?

10. **hít the bóoks** = study **(past = hit)**

- It's time to **hit the books.** If you don't, you're going to fail this class.
- Sorry I can't talk now. I have to **hit the books.**

Your Turn

Ask three students: Did a teacher or parent ever tell you that you needed to **hit the books**? If yes, why? If no, why wasn't it necessary to say this?

ALL CLEAR ?

11. **You can sáy THÁT agáin!** = I agree with you completely. Say this only when you are giving your opinion.

A: That test was really long.

B: **You can say that again!** I needed another hour.

Pronunciation Note: Use high intonation and stress on the word "that":

You can say ↗THAT ↘again!

Your Turn

Complete the dialogue.

A: ____!

B: **You can say THAT again!**

NEW EXPRESSION COLLECTION

pull an all-nighter	hand in/turn in something	take a test cold
burn the midnight oil	hand back	do well on a test
cram for	hand out	do well in school
stay up	handout	take a nap
in the nick of time	get a(n) __ on a test	hit the books
be in hot water	get good/bad grades	You can say that again!
his mind went blank		

Exercises

(See page 159 for pronunciation exercises for Lesson 2. Focus: Stress in Phrasal Verbs and Compound Nouns.)

1. Mini-Dialogues

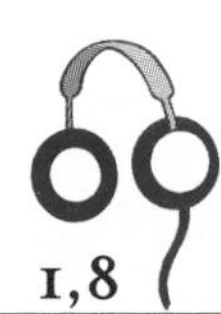

Read the sentences in Column A. Choose the *best* response from Column B. Not all responses can be used.

When checking this exercise in class, perform each mini-dialogue. One student should read an item from Column A, and another student should read the response from Column B.

1A

___ 1. Uh-oh! I forgot to pick her up from the airport.
___ 2. I slept only three hours last night.
___ 3. I'd like you to take out the handout I gave you yesterday.
___ 4. If you don't hit the books a little more, you'll be sorry.
___ 5. I ran all the way. Am I late?
___ 6. After I cram for a test, I forget everything I studied.
___ 7. How did he do on the test?
___ 8. Ssh! The baby's taking a nap.
___ 9. Can I ask you a question? Why did you take five points off my homework?

1B

a. So do I. That's the problem with studying at the last minute.
b. Sorry, I didn't know.
c. Because you turned this assignment in late.
d. Well, you're going to be in hot water when she sees you.
e. I can't find it. Can I have another one please?
f. Why don't you take a nap?
g. You're right. I'll try to work harder.
h. He always gets good grades.
i. I think he did pretty well.
j. No. You're lucky. You got here in the nick of time.

2A

___ 1. Let's pull an all-nighter together.
___ 2. English is a crazy language.
___ 3. I was so nervous that my mind went blank.
___ 4. His business is really successful.
___ 5. Where are you going?
___ 6. How did you do on the test?
___ 7. Did you study?
___ 8. Did you get your homework back?
___ 9. Did you get your tests back?

2B

a. You can say that again!
b. To bed. I can't stay up late again tonight. I'm really tired.
c. For how long? The whole test?
d. No, I have to take the test cold.
e. Sorry, I need to go now and hit the books.
f. I know, and that really surprises me because he didn't do well in school.
g. Uh-huh. She handed them back yesterday.
h. Uh-huh. She handed it back yesterday.
i. OK. But I didn't get an A.
j. Sorry, I can't. I need to sleep.

2. Grammar Practice

Follow the directions and complete the sentences.

Directions	Sentences
1. Add an article.	a. He's tired because he pulled ________ all-nighter. b. Ssh! The baby's taking ________ nap. c. I'm going to the library to hit ________ books. d. He's happy because he got ________ A again! e. She's unhappy because she got ________ C. f. They got to class in ________ nick of time.
2. Add a preposition.	a. He's happy because he got a good grade ________ his test. b. Her parents are proud of her because she's doing well ________ school. c. Half of the students did well ________ the test, and half didn't do well. d. I crammed ________ the test this morning. I'm sure I'll forget everything after the test. e. You got here ________ the nick ________ time! We were going to leave without you. f. I have to turn ________ my essay this morning, but after that I'll be free to meet you for coffee. g. She's ________ hot water with her boss because she forgot to tell him she had to leave work early.
3. Use past tense verbs.	a. They (cram) ________________ all night. b. They (stay up) ________________ all night. c. We (negative: be) ________________ in hot water. d. We (hand in) ________________ our paragraphs. e. We (negative: turn in) ________________ our homework. f. She always (get) ________________ high grades in school. g. After his parents talked to him, he (hit) ________________ the books. h. I (negative: take) ________________ the test cold. I studied a lot!

3. Error Correction

Find the errors and make corrections.

1. My report was due yesterday, but I handed in it today.
2. When the teacher handed it out the test, I was nervous.
3. I keep my teacher's hand outs organized in my binder.
4. When the teacher hand back our tests, the students always look worried.
5. I need to turn in my homework. I don't want to turn them in late.
6. Great! I got A!!!
7. When he was in his native country, he often takes naps in the afternoon.
8. She hit the books to study last night.
9. I hope I do well in my next test.
10. When we were teenagers, every Saturday night we are staying up late.

4. Choosing the Idiom

Alan and Charlie are roommates. They are pulling an all-nighter and talking about being tired. Fill in the blanks with the *best* possible expressions from the list on page 32. Pay special attention to how the expressions are used grammatically. You may need to consider verb tenses, subject-verb agreement, pronouns, etc. After you finish, practice reading the dialogue aloud.

You can say that again
pull an all-nighter
hand ___ in
turn ___ in
take a nap
do well in
hit the books
be in hot water
stay up

CHARLIE: What time is it?

ALAN: You don't want to know . . . It's 4:20.

CHARLIE: I'm so tired. I need to (1) ______________________ and then I'll study again.

ALAN: No you don't. Just get another cup of coffee.

CHARLIE: I don't want any more coffee. I just want my bed. I can't (2) ______________________ all night.

ALAN: Well, if you can't (3) ______________________, then you need to (4) ______________________ every night. Can you do that?

CHARLIE: I can try. It's better than having no sleep.

ALAN: OK then. Good-night. But you told me your paper is due at 10:00. Are you going to (5) ______________________ late?

CHARLIE: Probably. I'll tell the teacher I was sick.

ALAN: That's not very honest. What will happen if you (6) ______________________ late?

CHARLIE: Well, I'll probably (7) ______________________. I already missed a test and my teacher's not happy about that. I'm not (8) ______________________ that class.

ALAN: You're too busy. It's hard working full-time and going to school.

CHARLIE: (9) ______________________! Well, good night my friend.

ALAN: Good night. Sleep well. And I hope you won't be sorry tomorrow!

5. Sentence Writing

Read the paragraphs. Then write sentences about what you read. In each sentence, use at least one expression from the box. (**Bolded** words and phrases in the story represent where expressions can go.) Sometimes different expressions can be used. Underline the expressions that you use.

Notice that most of the sentences about Joe are in the present tense. This is because Joe is talking about his habits and his routine. Most of your sentences will be in the present tense. When you are talking about Joe, remember to put an 's' on present tense verbs.

Also, remember to pay attention to other grammar details: prepositions, articles, singular and plural nouns, etc.

Hi! I'm Joe. I think I have a lot of problems at school. I don't study very much. When I have a test, I usually **study** the night before. Sometimes **I don't get any sleep** before a test, so I'm tired and **forget everything**. And there are times when **I don't study at all**.

When my teachers **give us** our tests, I get really nervous. And I'm even more nervous when they **give us the tests back** and I see my grade. Sometimes **I don't pass. I have pretty low grades.**

Sometimes **my teachers collect** homework. Yes, you're right. I don't always do my homework, or I do it in a hurry **right before class**. My teachers know this and they tell me that **I'm in trouble** and that I need to **work hard and study more.**

They're right. You should see my notebook. My **papers** are very disorganized. Maybe next week I'll sit down and put things in order.

Well, that's all for now. I'm kind of tired and I need to **rest** before I watch TV.

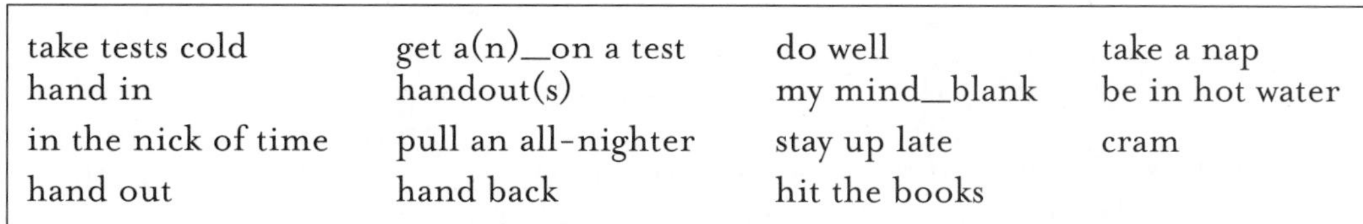

take tests cold	get a(n)__on a test	do well	take a nap
hand in	handout(s)	my mind__blank	be in hot water
in the nick of time	pull an all-nighter	stay up late	cram
hand out	hand back	hit the books	

Example: *When Joe has a test, he usually* <u>**stays up late**</u>.

6. Dictation

You will hear the dictation three times. First, just listen. Second, as you listen, write the dictation on a piece of paper. Skip lines. Third, listen again and check what you have written. Then look at the dictation in Appendix A on page 183.

Key Words: a paper, better-organized

7. Questions for Discussion and/or Writing

(For more detailed instructions, see Lesson 1, Exercise 7.)

Discussion: You can answer these questions orally in groups or in the *Walk and Talk* activity in Appendix B on page 186.

Writing: You can write your own answers to these questions, or you can write the responses that you received from students during the *Walk and Talk* activity.

Questions

1. Have you ever pulled an all-nighter? If no, why not? If yes, where? When? What class was it for? What did you do to stay awake?

See Appendix I on page 204 for Study Tips.

2. What kind of study habits do you (or did you) have as a student? That is, do you hit the books every night or do you cram at the last minute?
3. About tests: (a) What is the best way to study for a test on idioms and expressions? (b) Have you ever taken a test cold? If yes, explain the situation. (c) Has your mind ever gone blank during a test? If yes, explain what happened. (d) In your native country, do teachers often give surprise ("pop") quizzes? What is your opinion of surprise quizzes?
4. In your native country, can students turn in their work late? If they can turn their work in late, what is the penalty? That is, do they get a lower grade?
5. Describe a situation in which you were (or someone you know was) in hot water. What happened?

8. Role Play or Write a Dialogue

In the cartoon, Alan, Charlie, Annette, and their friend Liz are eating out at a pizza place. It is the day after Alan pulled an all-nighter and Charlie stayed up late. They are both exhausted. Annette feels better because she finally had a good-night's sleep. They are all talking about the pressures of being a student.

With a partner, write their conversation. Or, with three other students, role play the situation. Try to use some expressions from this lesson. Refer to or write on the board the New Expression Collection on page 28. Also, try to use other expressions that you know. But don't feel that it is necessary to have an idiom in every sentence.

Possible starting line: *You guys look really tired!*

9. Walk and Talk—BINGO

Ask the *Yes-No* questions on the BINGO card. Walk around the classroom and ask your questions. When a student says "Yes" or "Sometimes" write his or her name in the box. The first person to get ten or fifteen names is the winner.

Example:

A: *Do you usually stay up late?*
B: *No, I don't.*
A: *OK. Thank you.*

A: *Do you usually stay up late?*
B: *Yes, I do.*
A: *Great! What's your first name?*
. . . *How do you spell it?*

Do you usually stay up past midnight on weekends? ________	Do you usually stay up past 11:00 on weeknights? ________	Do you think it's good for students to have part-time jobs? ________	Are you ready to take a nap right now? ________	Are you going to hit the books tonight? ________
Did you hit the books the last time you had a test? ________	Did you ever take a test cold? ________	Do you usually cram before a test? ________	Did your parents check your homework when you were younger? ________	Do you think everyone should go to college? ________
Were you ever in hot water with a teacher? ________	Were you ever in hot water with a boss? ________	Free Space	Do you keep your teacher's handouts organized? ________	Do you get nervous when a teacher hands out or hands back a test? ________
Do you usually get things done just in the nick of time? ________	When you have a test, do you ever study with a group of classmates? ________	If you don't understand something, do you usually ask someone for help? ________	Do you take a dictionary with you everywhere you go? ________	When you read in English, do you have an idea when you see an idiom? ________
Did you ever drink a lot of coffee to help you pull an all-nighter? ________	Do you think you need to get good grades to get a good job? ________	Are you ready to use these new idioms when you speak or write? ________	Do you think students have too much pressure these days? ________	Is English very difficult for you? ________

10. Public Speaking

Sit on the Hot Seat

Answer questions from your classmates. See Appendix C on page 193 for sample questions.

Make a Speech

Prepare a five minute speech on one of the following topics. See Appendix D on page 194 for more information.

- How to deal with stress from school (and work)
- A typical school day in my native country
- A comparison between schools in my native country and in ________
- The advantages and disadvantages of wearing school uniforms

Note: Search the Internet if you need to get extra information.

Keep an Inventory
Add to:
Expression Clusters—Appendix E
Expression Collections—Appendices F and G

Review—Lessons 1 and 2

Collocation Match-Up

Collocations are special combinations of words that can be idioms or other phrases and expressions. Find collocations from *Lessons 1* and *2* by matching the words from Column A with words in Column B. (You will probably be able to make additional expressions that are not from Lessons 1 and 2. Put these in the box.)

A		B
1. get	cold feet	to go
2. calm	______________	went blank
3. pull	______________	good
4. be kind	______________	second thoughts
5. be just about ready	______________	up past midnight
6. be dying	______________	of nervous
7. do well	______________	off the picnic
8. be there in	______________	hot water
9. for	______________	down
10. hand	______________	to go
11. be in	______________	the books
12. be sort of	______________	B on a test
13. had	______________	an all-nighter
14. my mind	______________	naps
15. call	______________	in your report
16. get a	______________	cold feet √
17. couldn't	______________	on a test
18. take	______________	the nick of time
19. hit	______________	afford to buy a house
20. stay	______________	crazy

Additional Collocations

Review—Lessons 1 and 2

Crossword Puzzle

Across

1 I can't believe it! I got an 'A' and I took the test ___!

3 After I ___ in my homework, I left the class.

7 **A**: Doing crossword puzzles can take a lot of time.
B: You can say that ___!

8 They're together for ___. They have the perfect marriage.

10 I'm having second ___ about going because I'm really tired.

11 I'm sorry I can't see you today. I'm kind ___ busy.

12 He was just about ___ to ask her to marry him, but he saw her with another guy so he changed his mind.

14 They ___ in hot water yesterday because they got to work late.

Down

2 I ___ do well on the last test, so I'm going to study harder for the next test.

4 I can't pull an ___ because I need my sleep.

5 I crammed all night and now I'm ___ to take a nap.

6 I was absent yesterday. Can I please have the ___ about our speech?

9 She changed her mind about marrying him, so they're going to call ___ the wedding.

13 ___ down, do you really want to live here?

How are you doing? Complete the Self-Evaluation Questionnaire in Appendix H on page 203. Use the Study Tips in Appendix I on page 204.

Lesson 3

Are We Couch Potatoes?

Theme: Socializing with Friends; The Role of TV in Our Lives

Warm-Up

1. Look at the cartoon. What do you think a *couch potato* is?
2. Do you know any couch potatoes? Who? What kinds of TV programs do they watch? What kinds of snacks do they eat?
3. About how many hours of TV do you watch every day?
4. When you are invited to someone's home, do you usually take a gift? If yes, what types of gifts do you take?

Focused Listening

Before You Listen

Susan and Michael in the cartoon have just arrived at Ruth and Andy's house to watch some movies. What do you think they are saying?

As You Listen

Ⓐ Close your book. Listen to the conversation between the friends to find the answers to these questions.

Why are Susan and Michael visiting Ruth and Andy?
Does everyone agree that they are couch potatoes?

Ⓑ Listen again, but this time read the conversation as you listen.

I,II

Culture Note

In the United States, it is common to eat salted popcorn during a movie. What kind of snack is common in your native country?

ANDY:	Hi, guys! Come on in.
SUSAN:	Thanks. It's so good to see you! And here—we brought some popcorn.
RUTH:	Oh, you're so thoughtful! What a great idea! Here, let me take your coats. And come in and **make yourselves comfortable**. I'm so glad we can finally **get together**.
MICHAEL:	So are we. It's been such a long time. So tell me, what movies are we going to see tonight?
ANDY:	Well, we have two very old and famous ones—a comedy and a murder mystery. Want to guess what they are?
SUSAN:	Surprise us. But can we see the comedy first? I'**m in the mood for** something funny after a hard week at work.
RUTH:	Well, **that makes two of us. I don't feel like watching** anything serious. Hey—you know—I heard that it's *healthy* to laugh.
MICHAEL:	I heard that, too. There was something on TV about that—comedians were performing in hospitals.
ANDY:	Yeah, I saw that. It was really interesting.
SUSAN:	That reminds me. Yesterday my sister told me that Michael and I are couch potatoes because we watch so much TV. But do you think we're couch potatoes if we watch *good* shows?
MICHAEL:	Come on Susan. It doesn't matter *what* we watch—it's true that we **spend** a lot of **time sitting** on the couch and watching show after show.
RUTH:	Listen, there's no need to worry about being a couch potato tonight. We all need to relax, so let's watch a movie! The comedy first . . .

(After watching the two movies)

SUSAN: Well, it's getting late and we should be going.

MICHAEL: You two know how to pick good movies. Both were great. Thank you.

ANDY: Our pleasure. And it was really great seeing you. **Thanks for coming.**

SUSAN: **Thanks for having us.** Next time come over to our place and we'll surprise you with a couple of great classics.

RUTH: Sounds good. See you guys. Get home **safe and sound**!

After You Listen

(A) Below are details about the introductory conversations. Circle *T* for *true, F* for *false,* or *?* if you don't know.

1. The two couples watch movies together every weekend. T F ?
2. Susan has a good job. T F ?
3. Michael agrees with Susan's sister that they are couch potatoes. T F ?
4. Laughter is good for the health. T F ?
5. Susan invited Ruth and Andy to come over next weekend. T F ?

(B) **Guess the Meanings**
Below is a list of paraphrases of five of the idiomatic expressions in the conversation. On your own or with a partner, try to guess the five. To do this, make sure that what is written below would easily fit in the conversation.

Paraphrase	Idiomatic Expression
1. be with each other	______________________
2. I agree.	______________________
3. without any trouble	______________________
4. sit down and relax	______________________
5. don't want to	______________________

(C) Say the conversations in groups of four. Then have four students say the conversations in front of the class.

Understanding the New Expressions

Work with Others

If you're working with a partner or in a small group, read the short dialogues and examples for each expression aloud. Also, complete the Your Turn exercises together. For each expression, circle *Yes* or *No* to show if you understand. If you circled *No,* highlight or underline what is unclear, and ask questions for clarification.

Figure It out on Your Own

Read the short dialogues and examples for each expression. Also, complete the Your Turn exercises that don't need partners. Then, for each expression, circle *Yes* or *No* to show if you understand. If you circled *No,* highlight or underline what is still unclear, and ask questions in class for clarification.

ALL CLEAR ?

Pronunciation Note: Stress the second syllable with *self* or *selves* in reflexive pronouns.

1. **máke onesélf cómfortable = máke onesélf at hóme**
Hosts use these expressions to welcome their guests.

Grammar Note: Remember the reflexive pronouns—I/myself; you/yourself (singular); you/your<u>selves</u> (plural); he/himself; she/herself; we/our<u>selves</u>; they/<u>themselves</u>. "Self" is singular and "selves" is plural.

A: Hi, Annie! Why don't you sit down and **make yourself comfortable**? Can I get you a drink?
B: Thanks. I'd love one.

A: Hi everyone! Come on in and **make yourselves at home**.
B: Thanks. Where should we put our coats?

Related Expression: **hélp yoursélf (to something)** = serve yourself

- OK! Dinner's ready. It's a buffet, so **help yourself**!
- Welcome! Come on in and make yourselves comfortable. **Help yourselves to** a drink.

ALL CLEAR ?

2. **gét togéther** = join a person or people that you don't live with so that you can socialize (for dinner, to go to a movie—not for a vacation)

A: Do you want to **get together** this weekend?
B: I'd really like to, but let me check my calendar first. I'll call you back.

Grammar Note: Notice the use of *get together* "with" someone, *get together* "and" + verb, *get together* "for" + noun (not gerund):

- I want to **get together with** them sometime soon.
- We **got together (with them) and** had lunch.
- Let's **get together for** lunch.

Your Turn

Complete the dialogue with three possible answers.

A: What did you two do last weekend?
B: We got together with ______________________________.

We got together with ______________ and ______________.

We got together for ______________________________.

3. **be in the móod to** + ***verb*** = want (to do something)

be in the móod for + ***noun*** = want (something)

Grammar Note: It is not common to use a gerund with *be in the mood for.*

A: What do you want to do now?
B: I'**m in the mood to** dance. *OR*
I'**m in the mood for** a party. *OR*
I'**m not in the mood to** go dancing. Why don't we just watch a movie?

Your Turn

Complete the chart. Write sentences with words from the left column.

	(not) be in the mood to ___	(not) be in the mood for ___
dance/party	I'm in the mood to dance.	I'm in the mood for a party.
eat/hamburger		
(yesterday) go/movie		
listen to/classical music		

Similar Expressions: **be in a góod móod ≠ be in a bád móod**

Grammar Note: Don't put "to" or "for" after these expressions.

A: Do you want Chinese or Japanese food tonight?
B: Whatever you want.
A: You'**re in a good mood** today. Did something special happen?

A: Don't go near the boss today.
B: Why not?
A: He'**s in a** very **bad mood.**

4. Thát mákes TWÓ of us. = I feel the same way.

Note: This expression is often a response to different kinds of statements.

Pronunciation Note: The word *two* has the most meaning in this sentence. Give this word the most stress and highest intonation.

Expressing something you like or love	Expressing something you want	Expressing something you feel	Expressing an opinion
A: I love studying idioms.	A: I don't want to make a speech.	A: I need a break. I'm hungry.	A: I think English is a crazy language.
B: That makes two of us!	B: That makes two of us!	B: That makes two of us!	B: That makes two of us!

Similar Expressions: **So do I./Me, too./Neither __ I.**

With an affirmative statement:

A: I like old movies.
B: **That makes two of us.** *OR*
So do I. *OR*
Me, too.

With a negative statement:

A: I can't believe it.
B: **That makes two of us.** *OR*
Neither can I. *OR*
I can't either.

Your Turn

Complete the dialogues.

A: (affirmative statement) ______________________________
B: That makes two of us!

A: (negative statement) ______________________________
B: That makes two of us!

5. **féel líke __ing = be in the mood to** *do* something **(past = felt)**

A: What do you **feel like** doing?
B: I **feel like going** to a movie.
(**I'm in the mood to** go to a movie.)
OR
I **don't feel like going** out tonight. Let's stay home.
(**I'm not in the mood to** go out tonight. Let's stay home.)

A: Why didn't you cook tonight?
B: I **felt like ordering** a pizza. (I **didn't feel like cooking**.)
(I **was in the mood to** order a pizza./I **wasn't in the mood to** cook.)

Contrast:

A: How do you feel?
B: Fine./Happy./Tired.

Your Turn: Listening Challenge

Listen to the conversation and then complete the sentences in the chart.

	(not) feel like __ing	(not) be in the mood to __
eat out/go dancing	• She feels like eating out and going dancing. • He doesn't . . .	• She's in the mood to . . . • He isn't . . .
stay home/watch TV	• She • He	• She • He
cook	• She	• She

6. **spénd tíme** **doing** something (gerund—an activity) **(past = spent)**
on something (ON + noun)
with someone
at a place

Note: Use *spend time ON* + noun. We don't usually use *spend time ON* with gerunds.

- He **spends** a lot of **time working**.
- You need to **spend** more **time on** your homework, don't you think?
- She **doesn't spend** enough **time with** her kids.
- We **spent** a lot of **time at** the library last night.

Your Turn

Complete the sentences.

1. On weekends, I like to spend time ______________________________.
2. They didn't do well on the test because they didn't spend any time ______________________________.
3. She spends a lot of time on ______________________________, so she gets good grades.
4. He spends a lot of time on ______________________________ because he gets a lot of e-mail.
5. They spend a lot of time with ______________________________ because they're in love.
6. We work a lot, so we don't spend a lot of time at ______________________________.

7. **Thánks for cóming.** = Thanks for coming to our house.
Hosts use this expression when guests are leaving.

8. **Thánks for háving us (me).** = Thanks for inviting us (me) to your house.
Guests use this expression to respond to "Thanks for coming."

Grammar Note: "For" is a preposition. Always use a noun or gerund after this word.

A: **Thanks for coming.** Come again soon!
B: We will. **Thanks** a lot **for having us**.

Your Turn

In the column on the right, write what you would say in each situation. Use "Thanks for" or "Thank you for" with a gerund.

Situation	What you say
1. Someone helped you with your homework.	1. Thanks for helping me with my homework.
2. Someone took you home after work.	2.
3. Someone brought you a book that you forgot.	3.
4. Someone took care of your house or apartment while you were gone.	4.

9. sáfe and sóund = arrive somewhere safe, not hurt

- Have a good trip. Take care and get home **safe and sound**.
- She couldn't find her dog for two hours. But she finally found him **safe and sound** sleeping under the house.

Pronunciation Note: There are many word pairs with "and" in English. The word "and" is pronounced *'n* in fast speech.

Nouns	Verbs	Adjectives
bread 'n butter men 'n women peace 'n quiet pros 'n cons	wait 'n see forgive 'n forget	safe 'n sound short 'n sweet bright 'n early

NEW EXPRESSION COLLECTION

make yourself comfortable	be in the mood	spend time
make yourself at home	be in a good/bad mood	Thanks for coming.
help yourself	That makes two of us!	Thanks for having me.
get together	feel like	safe and sound

Exercises

(*See page 163 for pronunciation exercises for Lesson 3. Focus: Reduced Forms and Contractions.*)

1. Mini-Dialogues

Read the sentences in Column A. Choose the *best* response from Column B. Not all responses can be used.

When checking this exercise in class, perform each mini-dialogue. One student should read an item from Column A, and another student should read the response from Column B.

1A

___ 1. Come on in and make yourselves comfortable.
___ 2. What's wrong? You don't look very happy.
___ 3. She said she's really tired and she doesn't feel like cooking for us tonight.
___ 4. I'm scared to death of snakes and spiders.
___ 5. What do they need to do to help their kids?
___ 6. Thanks for coming!
___ 7. Did he call? What did he say?
___ 8. Where did you get that cake?

1B

a. I'm not. I'm in a really bad mood. I'll talk to you later.
b. Well, we can order a pizza, right?
c. That they got home safe and sound. Now you can relax.
d. Spend more time reading to them.
e. Thanks. Where should we put our coats?
f. I spent a lot of time at the beach.
g. From the kitchen table. She told us to help ourselves.
h. That makes two of us!
i. Thanks for having us!

2A

___ 1. Want to dance?
___ 2. I'm in the mood to see a movie.
___ 3. I'm in the mood for ice cream.
___ 4. How are you and your friend?
___ 5. I feel like getting some exercise.
___ 6. I can't remember how to spell all the irregular verbs.
___ 7. Why didn't you fly?

2B

a. Because I felt like driving.
b. Well, we got together for lunch and spent a lot of time talking. We're OK now.
c. I thought you were on a diet!
d. Oh, what do you want to see?
e. Good for you! And I feel like taking a nap!
f. Sorry. I'm not in the mood right now.
g. I want to spend more time with you.
h. Neither can I.

2. Grammar Practice

Follow the directions and complete the sentences.

Directions	Sentences
1. Add a preposition.	a. I want to get together ______________ them soon. b. Let's get together ______________ coffee. c. They made themselves ______________ home. d. Are you ______________ the mood ______________ pizza or Chinese food? e. Watch out! Our boss is ______________ a very bad mood. f. You're afraid of spiders? Well, that makes two ______________ us! g. In our class, we spend a lot of time ______________ grammar. h. They spend time ______________ each other on weekends. i. The kids spend time ______________ their grandparents' house during the summer. j. Thanks ______________ helping me with my homework.
2. Add a gerund. [*take a break; work in a garden*]	a. Thanks a million for __________________ me the free ticket to the concert! b. Do you feel like ________________ a break? I'm tired and I want to get some water. c. I spent a lot of time __________________ in my garden last weekend.
3. Add an article.	a. They're in __________ mood to go dancing. b. They're in __________ great mood tonight.
4. Add an irregular past tense verb.	a. They __________________ together last Saturday and had a great time. b. His dog walked into my house and immediately __________________ himself at home! c. On Sunday, when it was raining, she __________________ in the mood to read a good book. d. The weather was really warm last weekend and we __________________ like going swimming, so we went to the beach. e. The students in the idioms class __________________ a lot of time studying for the last test.
5. Add a reflexive pronoun. [Items *d* and *e* are quotations—the exact words that her mom said.]	a. We went into the living room and made __________________ comfortable. b. When I visit my aunt and uncle, I always make __________________ at home. c. When my cousins visited, they helped __________________ to everything in the kitchen! d. My mom said, "Susan, help __________________ to a drink." e. My mom said, "Susan and Michael, help __________________ to drinks."

3. Error Correction

Find the errors and make corrections.

1. When they visit us, they always make theirself comfortable at home. (2 errors)
2. I'm in a good mood to go out tonight.
3. I'm in the mood for go to a movie.
4. She feels like to go to a movie.
5. He's in the very good mood today.
6. She never feel like spend time in her homework. (3 errors)
7. Last night, they spend two hours to do their homework. (2 errors)
8. We get together with them and took a long walk last Sunday.
9. They safe and sound after their long trip.
10. Thanks for to come to my party.

1,14

4. Choosing the Idiom

Jack and Jill have been married for about fifty years. They are talking about how to spend the evening. Fill in the blanks with the *best* possible expressions from the list. Pay special attention to how the expressions are used grammatically. You may need to consider verb tenses, subject-verb agreement, pronouns, etc. After you finish, practice reading the dialogue aloud.

get together	spend all my time	in the mood to/for
feel like	that makes two of us	spend more time with

JACK: I'm bored.

JILL: So am I. What do you (1) ______________________ doing?

JACK: We could watch TV.

JILL: No. Remember, we promised each other that we'd watch no more than two hours a day. You don't want to become a couch potato, do you?

JACK: No, but I don't want to (2) ______________________ reading.

JILL: How about getting some more exercise?

JACK: Well, I'm never (3)______________________ get exercise.

JILL: (4) ______________, but you know we sit around too much. Did I tell you that Lucy wants to (5) ______________ with me three times a week and take walks?

JACK: That sounds like a good idea. You should (6) ______________ her.

JILL: You know you can come with us.

JACK: Jill, I'm really not (7) ______________ this conversation. Where's the remote?

5. Sentence Writing

Read the paragraphs. Then, write sentences about what you read. In each sentence, use at least one expression from the box. (**Bolded** words and phrases in the story represent where expressions can go.) Underline the expressions that you use.

Notice that most of the sentences about Dan are in the present tense. This is because Ann is talking about Dan's habits and his routine. Most of your sentences will be in the present tense. When you are talking about Dan, remember to put an 's' on present tense verbs.

Also, remember to pay attention to other grammar details: prepositions, articles, singular and plural nouns, etc.

Hi! I'm Ann. I want to tell you about my brother, Dan. He used to be a couch potato, but now he's a *mouse potato*. **He's always** at his computer. I think he's at his computer ten hours a day! He loves the Internet and I know that for half the day, **he searches** the Internet.

Every morning, he gets up and makes coffee. Then, **he gets into his special chair with his special pillow** and turns on his computer. I never talk to him before he has his coffee because **he's not very nice** before he has some caffeine. He makes me so mad that sometimes **I think I should move out** and **get** my own apartment. We're not very good roommates. We're very different. When **I want** chicken, **he wants** steak. When **I want to** go to the movies, **he wants to** stay home. When I want to **go out with** my friends, he wants me to stay home. I think he needs a wife!

make oneself comfortable	get together with	be in the mood for	be in the mood to
be in a (good) (bad) mood	feel like	spend time at	spend time ___ing

Example: *Dan always* **spends time at** *his computer.*

6. Dictation

You will hear the dictation three times. First, just listen. Second, as you listen, write the dictation on a piece of paper. Skip lines. Third, listen again and check what you have written. Then look at the dictation in Appendix A on page 183.

Key Words: couples, hosts, rainy

7. Questions for Discussion and/or Writing

(For more detailed instructions, see Lesson 1, Exercise 7.)

Discussion: You can answer these questions orally in groups or in the *Walk and Talk* activity in Appendix B on page 187.

Writing: You can write your own answers to these questions, or you can write the responses that you received from students during the *Walk and Talk* activity.

Questions

1. Do you know any couch potatoes? If yes, who? Are you one? How much TV do you watch every day? What kind of show is your favorite?
2. Do you think parents should limit how much TV their children watch? How many hours a day are OK? (Should parents limit how many hours a day children spend playing video games or using the Internet?)
3. How can parents prevent their children from watching TV shows that contain sex and violence?
4. When you watch TV in English, do you turn on the closed-captioning so that you can read what the people are saying? If yes, how does this help you?
5. When you see a movie that was made in a foreign language, do you prefer subtitles (words in your native language written at the bottom of the screen) or dubbing (words in your native language that are spoken)? Explain.
6. Who do you think holds the remote control more—men or women? Why?
7. Do you think it's possible to be addicted to the Internet? Do you know any *mouse potatoes*?

8. Role Play and Write a Speech

In the cartoon, people are attending a meeting of the "Couch Potato Club." The president is making a speech about how wonderful it is to watch at least seven hours of TV a day and eat a lot of "junk food" (potato chips, candy, etc.).

Work in small groups to write the president's speech. Use your imagination. Try to use some expressions from this lesson. Refer to or write on the board the New Expression Collection on page 47. Also, try to use other expressions that you know. But don't feel that it is necessary to have an idiom in every sentence.

After you have finished writing the speech, choose one student to give the speech to your group. After the speech, hold a question and answer session with the "president." (*Variation:* After practicing the speech in small groups, the couch potato "presidents" can take turns giving their speeches to the entire class.)

Possible starting line: *Today, I'm going to talk about why people should be couch potatoes.*

9. Word Search

Complete the expressions. Then, find the underlined words in the puzzle. The words can be spelled backwards. They can also be vertical (↕), horizontal (↔), or diagonal (↗) (↖).

1. Welcome Jan! Make ______________________________ comfortable!
2. You want a vacation? Well, that ______________________________ two of us!
3. We had a great time. Dinner was fantastic. Thanks for ____________________ us.
4. There was a big storm, but luckily everyone got home safe and ____________.
5. On rainy days, I like to spend a lot of time ______________________________ on the couch and watching TV.
6. I'm in the mood ______________________________ a party. Are you?
7. OK, everyone. It's time to eat! The food is on the table. It's a buffet, so help ______________________________.
8. We finally ______________________________ together last Saturday.
9. It was great having you over. Thanks for______________________________.
10. Do you feel like ______________________________ a movie tonight?
11. I'm in ______________________________ mood for pizza. How about you?
12. Why are you in such a bad ____________________? Come on, smile!

M O O D R D V F T N L O O U R
Y K O K Y O U R S E L F I N E
V N S W M R U D E G R R A W T
X C J E S G N I V A H F W N E
N H D L E G N I T T I S O T U
E W V N E S E V L E S R U O Y
Q G F B I D L I H B P T S O S
K O A R N D D X U F B O U X O
R T S E G M S O L Q O E X K R
M M Y J O J N R Z V G R X I M
B C O M I N G P G K T D Y D A
W J A E H T M D S N B J N C K
J E S O U N D T K N O Q N U E
Y B B R F H X M G Z F A P E S
K R B M A Y S A E L G Q B R N

10. Public Speaking

Sit on the Hot Seat

Answer questions from your classmates. See Appendix C on page 193 for sample questions.

Make a Speech

Prepare a five minute speech on one of the following topics. See Appendix D on page 194 for more information.

- What's good and bad about TV
- My favorite TV program (or video game, or movie)
- How TV programs (and/or movies, computer/video games, the Internet, etc.) help me learn English

Note: Search the Internet if you need to get extra information.

Keep an Inventory
Add to:
Expression Clusters–Appendix E
Expression Collections–Appendices F and G

Lesson 4

A Really Big Blackout

Theme: Preparing for and Dealing with an Emergency

Warm-Up

When the electricity (electric power) suddenly stops working, we say that the electricity "went out." And if this situation continues for a period of time, we say that there is a "blackout."

Have you ever been in a blackout? If yes, what were you doing when it happened? What did you and others do? How long did the blackout last?

Focused Listening

Before You Listen

Where are the two people in the cartoon? What do you think is their relationship? What do you think they are saying to each other?

As You Listen

(A) Close your book. Listen to the conversation between Carla and Dave to find the answers to these questions.

What's the problem and how big is it?
How did Dave get information about the problem?

1,16

(B) Listen again, but this time read the conversation as you listen.

till = until

CARLA: Dave! Finally! I'm so glad you called. Where were you?

DAVE: Sorry honey, I just checked my messages. It was a hard day. You know I'**m in charge of** a lot of these meetings. Are the lights still out?

CARLA: **They sure are!** And not just the lights. Everything is out. And I don't think my cell phone will stay charged for long. Do you have any idea how big this blackout is?

DAVE: No, but I'**m getting online** to find out right now. Wow Carla! You should see the map—it **looks like** the power **is out** in about five states!

CARLA: Does it say when they think it'**ll come back on**?

DAVE: Let's see . . . it says here that it might not come back on till tomorrow.

CARLA: Oh, no.

DAVE: I'm sorry I'm not there with you and Maggie.

CARLA: Me, too. I'm working by candlelight and it's very romantic.

DAVE: How can you work without electricity?

CARLA: Well, my laptop is still charged. I think I have about one more hour to work.

DAVE: And what **are** you **working on**?

CARLA: A report that's due tomorrow.

DAVE: Don't worry about it. I'm sure your boss doesn't expect you to work **in the dark**.

CARLA: I know, but it's something to do. Maggie'**s sound asleep**.

DAVE: I miss you both.

CARLA: I can't wait till you get home.

DAVE: Well, just two more days. And **chances are** the blackout will **be over** by then.

CARLA: I sure hope so! If it isn't, I'**ll go out of my mind**!

After You Listen

Ⓐ Below are details about the introductory conversation. Circle *T* for *true,* *F* for *false,* or *?* if you don't know.

1. Carla and Dave both have jobs. T F ?
2. Dave knew about the blackout before he called. T F ?
3. Maggie was afraid when the lights went out. T F ?
4. Carla's boss will be angry if she doesn't finish her report. T F ?
5. Dave will be home the day after tomorrow. T F ?

Ⓑ **Guess the Meanings**

Below is a list of paraphrases of five of the idiomatic expressions in the conversation. On your own or with a partner, try to guess the five. To do this, make sure that what is written below would easily fit in the conversation.

Paraphrase	Idiomatic Expression
1. probably	____________________
2. responsible for	____________________
3. end	____________________
4. appears (seems) to be	____________________
5. go crazy	____________________

Ⓒ Say the conversation in pairs. Then have two students say the conversation in front of the class.

Understanding the New Expressions

Work with Others

If you're working with a partner or in a small group, read the short dialogues and examples for each expression aloud. Also, complete the Your Turn exercises together. For each expression, circle *Yes* or *No* to show if you understand. If you circled *No,* highlight or underline what is unclear, and ask questions for clarification.

Figure It out on Your Own

Read the short dialogues and examples for each expression. Also, complete the Your Turn exercises that don't need partners. Then, for each expression, circle *Yes* or *No* to show if you understand. If you circled *No,* highlight or underline what is still unclear, and ask questions in class for clarification.

1. **be in chárge (of)** = Be the main person responsible for making sure that (a) people get things done or (b) something gets done.

   Grammar Note: Remember to use a noun or gerund after the preposition *of.*

   - She got a great new job with a lot of responsibility. In fact, she's going to **be in charge of** about 50 people!
   - Listen, there's a lot to do to prepare for the party. I'll do the invitations. Who wants to **be in charge of** the food? And who wants to **be in charge of** clean**ing** up after the party?

   A: Who'**s in charge** here?
   B: I'**m in charge.**
   A: Are you the babysitter?
   B: Uh-huh.
   A: Well, you're not doing your job. The neighbors are complaining about all the noise.

Your Turn

Look at the list on the left. Write *who is in charge* on the right.

	Who's in charge?
1. your country	______________
2. your job	______________
3. your family	______________
4. paying the bills in your family	______________
5. cleaning your house or apartment	______________
6. your class	______________
7. an airplane	______________

2. **They súre ÁRE!** = They definitely are! Absolutely!
   Use this expression when you want to give a very strong "Yes!" in answer to a question.

   Pronunciation Note:
   Say this expression with feeling. Use strong stress and rising and falling intonation on the last word, *are.* (The verb *BE* can be stressed when it is the last word in a sentence.)

Grammar Note: You can use this expression with different subjects and the verb *BE* in various tenses.

Present Tense	Past Tense	Future Tense
Am I a good student? You sure are! Are you worried? I sure am! Is Carla a good wife? She sure is!	Was I impolite? You sure were! Were you scared during the earthquake? We sure were! Was Dave busy? He sure was!	Are they coming to the party next week? They sure are! Are you going to prepare emergency supplies? We sure are!

Grammar Note: You can form similar expressions with **sure** by using different subjects + *DO, CAN, WILL,* and other auxiliary verbs.

Present Tense	Past Tense	Future Tense
Do you think English is hard? I sure do! Does he think English is hard? He sure does! Can they speak English? They sure can!	Did you do your homework? I sure did! Could you run fast when you were a kid? I sure could!	Will you be here next year? I sure will! Will you come over if I need help? I sure will!

3. **gét (gót) onlíne** = get on the Internet

A: I need to check my e-mail. Do you know where I can **get online**?

B: Well, there's an Internet café around the corner. Or, you can use a computer at the library.

Other uses of the word ***online****, which means "on the Internet:"*

A: Where did you get your information about emergency supplies?

B: I did some research **online.** *OR*
I found it **online.**

Contrast: When you go to the back of a line, such as at a bank, you **get in line** or **get on line**. In different parts of the United States, people use "in" or "on." These expressions have spaces between the words. "Online," when related to the Internet, is one word.

4. **It lóoks like . . .** = It seems/appears; What someone *sees* or *knows* gives the impression that . . .

Grammar Note: Use a subject and verb after *"It looks like."*

- From the map, **it looks like** five states are having a blackout.
- **It looks like** there's going to be a big storm. Do we have a flashlight and batteries?
- You have three A's and a B. **It looks like** you'll get an A.
- They aren't happy. **It looks like** they're going to get a divorce.

Contrast: X **looks like** someone or something else = resemble physically

When the expression has this meaning, it is followed by a noun.

- He **looks like** his father. They have the same eyes.
- She **doesn't look like** her mother.

Similar Expression: **It sóunds like . . .** = What someone *hears* gives the impression that . . .

Grammar Note: Use a subject and verb after *"It sounds like."*

A: How was the party?
B: Oh, the music was fantastic and everyone danced all night. And the food was great, too.
A: **It sounds like** you had a great time.

Contrast: X **sounds like** someone or something else

When the expression has this meaning, it is followed by a noun.

A: Hi, Ruth.
B: No, it's Christine.
A: Christine? You **sound like** your mother! I can't believe it!
B: Everyone says that. Hold on a second and I'll get her.

Your Turn

Add a sentence to each column in the chart.

It looks like + **subject/verb**	_ *look(s) like* + **noun**	*It sounds like* + **subject/verb**	_ *sound(s) like* + **noun**
a. It looks like it's going to rain.	a. He looks like his father.	a. It sounds like you had a great time.	a. You sound like your mother.
b. ______________	b. ______________	b. ______________	b. ______________

Note: You can create similar sentences with other verbs related to the senses: feel like/taste like/smell like.

It feels/tastes/smells like + **subject/verb**	_ *feel, taste, smell(s) like* + **noun**
a. *It feels like it's going to snow.*	a. *He feels like an old man.*
b. *It tastes like it's very fresh.*	b. *It tastes like chicken, but it's fish.*
c. *It smells like someone's smoking.*	c. *It smells like smoke.*

5. go óut/be óut/come back ón (related to electricity or electric power)

the electricity / the power ⟶ **goes out** ⟶ **is out** ⟶ **comes back on**

- When we have big storms around here, the power often **goes out.**
- When the power **is out,** we get our flashlights, listen to the radio, talk to each other, take walks, and go to bed early.
- I'm sorry I didn't do my homework. The power **was out/went out** in my neighborhood last night.
- The power **went out** for just a second, and then it **came back on.**
- Uh-oh! The power **went out**!
  The electricity **went out**!

Note: The power goes out when you don't control it. If you do control the power where you live, you can turn it on and off. You can say, "The electrician turned the power off while he was working."

6. **wórk on (something)** = do work on a particular task or project

Grammar: Remember to use a noun or gerund after the preposition ***on***.

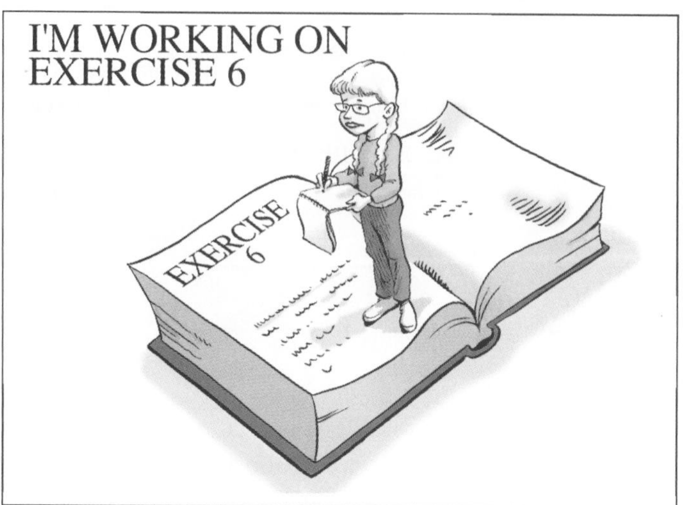

- OK, everyone. Now it's time to **work on** Exercise 3.
- He's **working on** his book this weekend, so he's busy.
- They'**re working on** their research project this week because it's due next Monday.
- We'**re working on** the problem and we expect to have a solution very soon.
- I **worked on** my essay for five hours!
- You need to **work on improving** your grades.

Your Turn: Listening Challenge

Listen to each situation. Then, write a sentence about what each person is working on. Be sure to use the expression *work on* + a noun or gerund. (Different sentences are possible.)

1. They ____.
2. He ____.
3. She ____.

7. **in the dárk** = in a place where there is no light

Note: This is a phrase, but not really an idiom because it describes a place that is truly dark. The expression described below, "be in the dark," is a true idiom.

- Turn on a light! How can you work **in the dark**?
- Lots of animals can see **in the dark**.
- Does your camera work **in the dark**?

Similar Expressions:

(1) **be in the dárk (about)** = not know anything about something

A: Did you know about the surprise party?
B: No, I had no idea. I **was** completely **in the dark**.

Don't **be in the dark about** {
your health.
what's in your food.
how to prepare for an emergency.
the dangers of global warming.

(2) **be afráid of the dárk** = have a fear of being in a dark place

The children **are afraid of the dark**, so they have a nightlight in their room.

8. **be sóund asléep** = be in a deep sleep

- Teacher: Andy, can you answer number 3? . . . Oh, it looks like Andy **is sound asleep**. Hmmm . . . Let's wake him up!

A: Did you hear the thunder last night?
B: No. I didn't hear a thing. I **was sound asleep**.

9. **chánces are** = probably

Note: This expression doesn't change. It is always used in the plural, and always used in the present tense.

A: Where's Andy?
B: He was asleep in class yesterday, and he had a fever last night. **Chances are**, he's home in bed.

Your Turn

Think of people in a time zone far away from where you are right now. What time is it there? Write what you think they are probably doing right now. Follow the example.

Example: It's 11:30 at night in Brazil right now. Chances are, my friends are at a party. (OR: Chances are, my parents are sleeping.)

____

____

____

____

____

ALL CLEAR ?

10. be óver = end

Notes:

(1) Only things that last for a period of time (have duration) can be over: a relationship, a strike, a war, a movie, a TV program, a semester, a game, a party, etc.

(2) A person cannot be *over.* You cannot say "I'm over." Instead, say "I'm done" or "I'm finished."

A: I'll do my homework when this show **is over**.
B: No, you'll do your homework right now. Turn off the TV.

- Call me when the party'**s over**, and I'll pick you up.
- When vacation **is over**, I'm always ready to get back to work.
- The day after their honeymoon **was over**, they went back to work.
- When the Olympics **were over**, the athletes all went home.
- The program **will be over** at 9:00, and I'll call you back then.

Contrast: **be dóne (with); be fínished (with)**

- I'**m done** (**with** my homework).
- We'**re finished** (**with** our test).

11. **gó óut of one's mínd(s) (with)** = go (become) crazy

A: I have so much to do that I'**m going out of my mind**.
(*OR:* I'**m going out of my mind with** all this work.)

B: Maybe you need to take a break.

Grammar Notes:

(1) This expression is often followed by a gerund.

He's **going out of his mind** { **living** here. / **working** there. / **worrying** about money. / **trying** to find an apartment. }

(2) When you have a plural subject, make "mind" plural.

They **went out of their minds** trying to get a reservation.

Similar expression: **be óut of one's mínd** = be crazy

Note: First people "go" out of their minds, and then they "are" out of their minds.

- You'**re out of your mind**! Why are you driving so fast in this traffic?
- They'**re out of their minds.** How can they ride their bikes at night without lights?

Other expressions that mean crazy: **be/go nuts, bananas, insane, off one's rocker**

ALL CLEAR ?

Culture Note

In the United States, pointing to your head and making a circular motion with your index finger shows that you think someone is crazy. What gesture is used in your native country?

NEW EXPRESSION COLLECTION		
be in charge of	X sounds like	be sound asleep
They sure are!	go out	chances are
get online	be out	be over
it looks like	come back on	be done/finished with
X looks like	work on	go out of one's mind
it sounds like	in the dark	

Exercises

(*See page 166 for pronunciation exercises for Lesson 4. Focus: Intonation in Statements and Questions.*)

1. Mini-Dialogues

Read the sentences in Column A. Choose the *best* response from Column B. Not all responses can be used.

When checking this exercise in class, perform each mini-dialogue. One student should read an item from Column A, and another student should read the response from Column B.

1A

___ 1. Were you afraid of the dark when you were a kid?

___ 2. Why are you so late?

___ 3. I hate to tell you this, but it looks like we have to cancel our plans. Johnny has a fever.

___ 4. During the hurricane, hundreds of people stayed in the high school gym. It was very organized.

___ 5. Can we talk?

___ 6. Who do you look like more, your mother or your father?

1B

a. I missed my stop because I was sound asleep the whole time I was on the train.

b. Maybe later. I'm going out of my mind with all this work.

c. I sure was! And I was sure that a monster lived in my closet!

d. It's hard to say. What do *you* think?

e. Chances are he's afraid of the dark.

f. That's good to hear. Who was in charge? The Red Cross?

g. I'm so sorry. I know the flu is going around. Do you think that's what he has?

2A

___ 1. I don't have any emergency supplies, but I need to get some.

___ 2. Are they ready to get married?

___ 3. Chances are there's going to be a big earthquake in the next thirty years.

___ 4. What's wrong? You look upset.

___ 5. The electricity went out when he was on the train. Everyone had to walk through the tunnel in the dark.

___ 6. What's the homework for next week?

2B

a. How do you know? How can you predict the future?

b. I am. I spent almost an hour in line waiting to get online at the library.

c. Well, we need to work on our reports and study for a test. But I'm in the dark about what'll be on it. Do you know?

d. You sound like me. I always say that, but I keep saying I'll do it tomorrow.

e. She sure is!

f. Really? That sounds like a terrible experience.

g. They sure are!

2. Grammar Practice

Follow the directions and complete the sentences.

Directions	Sentences
1. Add a preposition.	a. Who's __________ charge __________ hiring where you work? b. I'm working __________ my resume because I need to apply for a new job. c. I have no idea what happened. I'm completely __________ the dark. d. They're not afraid __________ the dark, so you can turn out the lights. e. He's going out __________ his mind trying to fix his computer. f. The power went out at 3:00 and came back __________ at around 5:00.
2. Add a gerund.	a. Who's in charge of __________ emergency supplies? b. We're working on __________ better grades, so we study all the time. c. She's going out of her mind __________ about him all the time.
3. Add a form of the verb *BE*.	a. When I was a kid, my teacher told me I __________ in charge of erasing the board. b. I'll pay the bills this month, but starting next month, you __________ in charge of paying the bills. c. When she asked if I was ready for a vacation, I said, "I sure __________!" d. I know he __________ completely in the dark about the party because when we said "Surprise!," he looked shocked. e. We couldn't cook last night because the power __________ out and we have an electric stove. f. The thieves thought the people __________ sound asleep, but they (negative) __________, and they called the police. g. When the movie __________ over, let's get a cup of coffee. h. I thought he __________ out of his mind when he said he was going to marry her, but I was wrong. She's really great and I like her now.

3. Error Correction

Find the errors and make corrections.

1. I'm over with my homework.
2. Chances will be that the weather will be better tomorrow.
3. I went out my mind with all that work last week.
4. When the power come back on at 5 o'clock, everyone clapped.
5. When I asked him what he was doing, he said he was working in his application.
6. We're in dark about that. Tell us what happened.
7. He's only 12, but he looks just like his father on the phone.
8. They didn't call to say they were late, so we went out of our minds to worry about them.
9. It sound likes you had a great vacation.
10. We got online at the bus stop.

4. Choosing the Idiom

Melissa is talking to her Uncle Steve about her new job. Fill in the blanks with the *best* possible expressions from the list. Pay special attention to how the expressions are used grammatically. You may need to consider verb tenses, subject-verb agreement, pronouns, prepositions, etc. Not all of the expressions can be used. After you finish, practice reading the dialogue aloud.

be over	be sound asleep	be in charge of
I sure am	go out of __ mind	be in the dark about
get online	it looks like	be afraid of the dark
work on	it sounds like	chances are

MELISSA: Uncle Steve, I got it! They just called! Finally! I (1) ______________ waiting to hear from them.

STEVE: Wow! Congratulations! They picked the right person, that's for sure.

MELISSA: Thanks. And listen to this—I'm going to (2) ______________ the emergency preparedness office! From what my boss said, (3) ______________ I'm going to have a lot of responsibilities.

STEVE: Are you worried?

MELISSA: (4) ______________! I've never been anyone's boss before.

STEVE: Take it easy Melissa. You'll do fine. When do you start?

MELISSA: Next Monday. And I'm really nervous. I (5) ______________ where to go and what to do.

STEVE: Don't worry. (6) ______________ someone will explain everything to you. And don't forget, you know all about hurricanes, floods, tornados, and earthquakes. You're quite an expert.

MELISSA: I guess I am. Five years ago, after the big hurricane, I (7) ______________ to learn everything I could about emergencies. And here I am today with this job! I can't believe it!

STEVE: You keep saying that. And it *is* pretty amazing that you're in this profession considering that you (8) ______________ when you were a little kid.

MELISSA: Yeah, pretty amazing.

STEVE: So what are you going to do now?

MELISSA: Hmm . . . well, (9) ______________ it's going to rain, but I'm going to go out anyway and take a walk.

STEVE: Good idea. Listen, I have a meeting now. But when it (10) ______________, I'll pick you up and take you out to dinner to celebrate. How would you like that?

5. Sentence Writing

Read the paragraphs. Then, write sentences about what you read. In each sentence, use at least one expression from the box. (**Bolded** words and phrases in the story represent where expressions can go.) Underline the expressions that you use.

Notice that when Sophie is talking about right now, she uses the present continuous tense with action verbs, and she uses the present tense with non-action verbs. When she is talking about the past, she uses the past tense. When you write your sentences with expressions, pay special attention to the verb tenses.

Also, remember to pay attention to other grammar details: prepositions, articles, singular and plural nouns, etc.

Hi! I'm Sophie. Do you want to know what we're doing? Well, we're college students and we're volunteering at an elementary school. We're **working hard collecting** earthquake supplies. We decided that I should **be the boss** because I'm the oldest. That's fine with me because I kind of like telling everyone what to do.

Anyway, **you can see that** this is a lot of work. But that's OK. Three of us are doing the work, so **we'll probably** be finished in a day or two. When we started, **we had no idea** about what supplies to get. But we **looked on the Internet** and found a website with a lot of information about what to do before, during, and after an earthquake.

Yesterday two of us went shopping for canned food, flashlights, batteries, blankets, and other things at a discount store. It was so crowded, **it made me crazy** because I don't have a lot of free time. But we got almost everything we needed.

You're probably thinking that **what we're doing is** a lot of work—and it is. But we're happy to do it. Everyone wants the kids to be safe. And do you think the teachers and parents are happy to have our help? Well, **they definitely are!**

work on	be in the dark about	chances are
go out of _ mind	get online	be in charge
it sounds like	they sure are	it looks like

Example: *Sophie and her friends* **are working on** *getting earthquake supplies.*

6. Dictation

You will hear the dictation three times. First, just listen. Second, as you listen, write the dictation on a piece of paper. Skip lines. Third, listen again and check what you have written. Then look at the dictation in Appendix A on page 183.

Key Words: business, Maggie, candlelight, lasted

7. Questions for Discussion and/or Writing

(For more detailed instructions, see Lesson 1, Exercise 7.)

Discussion: You can answer these questions orally in groups or in the *Walk and Talk* activity in Appendix B on page 188.

Writing: You can write your own answers to these questions, or you can write the responses that you received from students during the *Walk and Talk* activity.

Questions

1. Do you use the Internet? If yes, how often do you get online? How often do you check your e-mail? What kinds of Web sites do you like to visit? Do you go to sites that are in your native language or in English, or both?
2. Do you have any projects that you're working on now? If yes, what are they? What are you planning to work on in the future?
3. What are you going to do when this program or semester or school year is over? How do you think you'll feel?
4. What kinds of things bother you? In other words, what makes you go out of your mind?
5. Are you from an area where there are natural disasters such as hurricanes, tornadoes, floods, or earthquakes? If yes, describe an experience you or someone you know had with an event.
6. What do you think people should do to prepare for an emergency situation? Have you already done this preparation or are you planning to?

8. Role Play or Write a Dialogue

In the cartoon, Carla and Dave are having dinner. Dave just got back from his trip. They are talking about experiences that people had during the blackout, which lasted 28 hours.

These are the experiences that some people had when the power was out:

- Carla's brother was on a train and had to walk through a tunnel.
- Dave's best friend was in an elevator.
- Their neighbors were in a crowded movie theater.
- They heard on the news that hospitals used emergency generators.

Other people were at work (using their computers), driving, at airports, in restaurants, shopping, etc.

With a partner, write Carla and Dave's conversation. Try to use some expressions from this lesson. Refer to or write on the board the New Expression Collection on page 65. Also, try to use other expressions that you know. But don't feel that it is necessary to have an idiom in every sentence.

Possible starting line: *People have so many stories about where they were during the blackout!*

9. Unscramble and Find the Secret Message

Unscramble the words to make sentences with the expressions from this lesson. Then, find the secret message at the bottom of the page.

WOH'S NI AEGRHC RHEE

I RESU MA

EW ESRU ERA

LET'S EGT ONINLE AT AN TTENERIN ACFE

IT SOOLK KELI WE SEMDIS ETH BUS

SEH KSOOL KILE HER RSITES

TI SDSNOU LIEK UOY DHA FUN

UYO SDNUO ELKI EM

OYU NUOSD ILEK UOY EHAV A OCDL

EH SEEDN OT RWOK ON IHS KMOWHERO

I SWA NI EHT RDAK BUTOA TATH

CESHACN RAE HTE TSOMR IWLL EB ERVO OSON

M'I OS ORBDE, I'M IGGNO TUO FO YM MNID

OND'T WROK NI HET KADR

Secret Message:

10. Public Speaking

Sit on the Hot Seat

Answer questions from your classmates. See Appendix C on page 193 for sample questions.

Make a Speech

Prepare a five minute speech on one of the following topics. See Appendix D on page 194 for more information.

- How to prepare for an emergency
- What to do during and after an earthquake
- An experience I or others had (with a blackout, a storm, etc.)

Note: You may want to choose your topic depending on where you live because people face different dangers in different places.

Search the Internet if you need to get extra information.

Keep an Inventory
Add to:
Expression Clusters—Appendix E
Expression Collections—Appendices F and G

Review—Lessons 3 and 4

Collocation Match-Up

Collocations are special combinations of words that can be idioms or other phrases and expressions. Find collocations from *Lessons 3* and *4* by matching the words from Column A with the words in Column B. (You will probably be able to make additional expressions that are not from Lessons 3 and 4. Put these in the box.)

A		B
1. make yourself	at home	mood
2. help yourselves	______	to watch TV
3. work on	______	working on an application
4. get together	______	having me over
5. be in the mood	______	the dark
6. be in the mood for	______	are
7. smell like	______	to a drink
8. be in a very bad	______	thinking about that
9. feel like	______	asleep
10. spent time	______	at home ✓
11. thanks for	______	hiring
12. safe and	______	a cup of hot tea
13. be sound	______	around 11:00
14. we sure	______	an application
15. it looks like	______	smoke
16. be afraid of	______	nuts
17. be in charge of	______	taking a nap
18. be over	______	it's going to be impossible
19. go out of your mind	______	sound
20. go	______	and have lunch

Additional Collocations

Review—Lessons 3 and 4

Crossword Puzzle

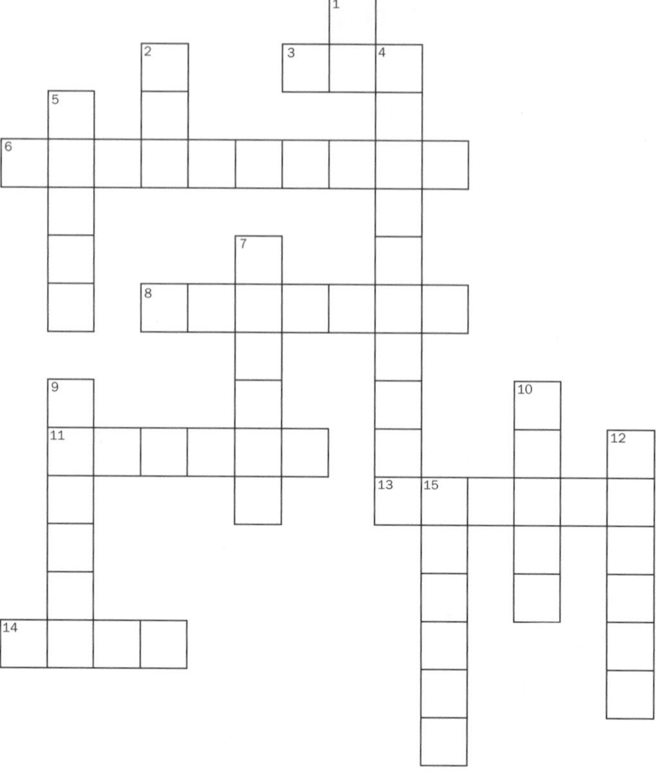

Across

3 We ___ together last week with them. We had a great time.

6 It's great to see you two! Sit down and make ___ comfortable!

8 We're not very happy here. ___ are we're going to move next month.

11 Thanks for ___ me. I had a great time tonight.

13 It ___ like you're working really hard on your English.

15 When all of her tests ___ over, she celebrated by going out to dinner.

Down

1 I'm in the mood ___ see a movie. Want to join me?

2 I think I'm in the mood ___ a quiet weekend. No parties for me!

4 The two dogs came in and made ___ comfortable on the couch!

5 Everyone got home safe and ___ during the storm.

7 I feel like ___ a long walk. It's a beautiful day.

9 They want to give their son some responsibilities. So the little boy is in ___ of feeding his cat.

10 All of the students were going out of their ___ trying to remember how to spell all those words.

12 Ssh! He's sound ___ and I don't want to wake him up.

14 Where's the computer? I want to get ___ and learn more about that.

How are you doing? Complete the Self-Evaluation Questionnaire in Appendix H on page 203. Use the Study Tips in Appendix I on page 204.

Lesson 5

Workaholic Mom

Theme: Work Pressure

Warm-Up

A workaholic is a person who is addicted to work. What kinds of problems do you think workaholics face?

Focused Listening

Before You Listen

What kind of job do you think the woman has? The woman is a workaholic. What do you think she is saying on the phone?

As You Listen

1,21

(A) Close your book. Listen to the conversation between Rosemary and Pat to find the answers to these questions.

What is their relationship?

What is the problem and what is the final decision?

(B) Listen again, but this time read the conversation as you listen.

ROSEMARY:	Thanks for the invitation honey, but I'll have to **take a rain check**.
PAT:	But Mom, it's your birthday!
ROSEMARY:	I know, I know. But I'**m swamped with** work. It won't **make a difference** if we go next week.
PAT:	Yes it will! It won't be your birthday next week. I want to take you to dinner *on* your birthday, not after.
ROSEMARY:	Well, you know I'd love to **take you up on** your invitation, but . . .
PAT:	But what?
ROSEMARY:	OK. I'll work late tonight and tomorrow night and **get** this project **over with**, and that way I'll be free Thursday night.
PAT:	Oh, thanks Mom! Wow! I didn't know it would be so hard to **talk you into going** out and **celebrating**.
ROSEMARY:	Well, you know me. I have so much responsibility now that I have this new position.
PAT:	I know you're really busy, but you should make time to celebrate. **After all**, your birthday comes only once a year, right?
ROSEMARY:	Right. So tell me, where do you want to eat?
PAT:	I **have** two special places **in mind**, but I keep **going back and forth**. I'll decide tomorrow and make a reservation. It's going to be a surprise.
ROSEMARY:	Well! Now, I'**m** really **looking forward to** Thursday!
PAT:	And there's going to be one more surprise, but I'm not going to tell you till we'**re through with** dinner.
ROSEMARY:	Another surprise? Pat, tell me now! Are you really going to make me wait?

After You Listen

Ⓐ Below are details about the introductory conversation. Circle *T* for *true,* *F* for *false,* or *?* if you don't know.

1.	Rosemary has a new job.	T	F	?
2.	Pat is going to pay for dinner.	T	F	?
3.	Rosemary doesn't want to go out to dinner.	T	F	?
4.	Pat has invited other relatives to the dinner.	T	F	?
5.	Pat and her mother have a good relationship.	T	F	?

Ⓑ **Guess the Meanings**

Below is a list of paraphrases of five of the idiomatic expressions in the conversation. On your own or with a partner, try to guess the five. To do this, make sure that what is written below would easily fit in the conversation.

Paraphrase	Idiomatic Expression
1. accept	______________________
2. convince/persuade	______________________
3. changing my mind	______________________
4. finished/done with	______________________
5. go at another time	______________________

Ⓒ Say the conversation in pairs. Then have two students say the conversation in front of the class.

Understanding the New Expressions

Work with Others

If you're working with a partner or in a small group, read the short dialogues and examples for each expression aloud. Also, complete the Your Turn exercises together. For each expression, circle *Yes* or *No* to show if you understand. If you circled *No,* highlight or underline what is unclear, and ask questions for clarification.

Figure It out on Your Own

Read the short dialogues and examples for each expression. Also, complete the Your Turn exercises that don't need partners. Then, for each expression, circle *Yes* or *No* to show if you understand. If you circled *No,* highlight or underline what is still unclear, and ask questions in class for clarification.

Culture Note

Origin of "take a rain check"—At the end of the 18th century in the United States, when a baseball game had to be canceled because of rain, people were given a "rain check" that they could use as a ticket at a future game.

1. **táke a ráin check** = get a chance to accept an invitation at a future time

A: Can you come over for dinner tonight?
B: I'm sorry, I can't. I have a class. Can I **take a rain check**?

A: Didn't they invite him to go swimming?
B: Uh-huh. But he has a cold, so he had to **take a rain check**.

Contrast: **gíve (somebody) a ráin check/ásk for a ráin check**

A: Can you come over for dinner tonight?
B: I'm sorry, I can't. Can you **give me a rain check** for next week?

- They invited us for dinner tonight, but I **asked for a rain check** because I'm tired.

Your Turn

With a partner, complete the sentences with *take, give,* or *ask for.* Use each verb once. Pay attention to verb tenses.

1. When they invited us to dinner, we ________________ a rain check because we were too tired to go out.
2. A: Can you come over for dinner tonight?

   B: I'd love to, but I already have plans for tonight. Can I ________________ a rain check?
3. A: Can you come over for dinner tonight?

   B: I'd love to, but I already have plans for tonight. Can you ________________ me a rain check?

2. **be swámped (with)** = Have a large amount of something, or have a large amount of something to do, especially work.

ALL CLEAR ?

Note: A *swamp* is an area of land with a lot of mud because the land is full of water. Just like a swamp is full of water, people can be full of work—they are "swamped."

He's in a swamp.

He's swamped with work.

- Sorry. I can't go out tonight. I'**m swamped**.
I'**m swamped with** homework.
- When they announced the schedule for the English program, they **were swamped with** requests.

Similar Expressions: **be drówning in wórk, be swímming in wórk, be up to one's éyeballs (éars) in wórk**

- Don't call them tonight. They'**re drowning in work.**
swimming in work.
up to their ears in work.

3. **It dóesn't máke a dífference (to someone). = It makes no difference (to someone).** = It doesn't matter. It has no effect (on someone).

ALL CLEAR ?

Question	Response
Do you want chicken or fish tonight?	It doesn't make a difference./It makes no difference. I like both.
Should we leave Friday or Saturday?	It doesn't make a difference./It makes no difference. We can leave any time.

Note: You can use other negative forms:
It *didn't* make a difference.
It *won't* make a difference.

- We tried to talk to her, but **it didn't make a difference**. She didn't listen to us.
- Let's leave Saturday. **It won't make a difference.**

Contrast: **máke a dífference** = be important, matter, have an effect (sometimes on society)

- I painted my room blue and it **made a big difference**.
- She wants to **make a difference**. That's why she decided to be a doctor.
- It's important to do something that **makes a difference**. Maybe you should do some volunteer work in your community.

4. **gét something óver with** = Do something that you don't enjoy, so you won't have to do it later.

A: Some people say, "Don't do tomorrow what you can do today." I say, "Don't do today what you can do tomorrow."

B: I'm different. When I have something to do, like cleaning or work, I like to **get it over with**. Then, I can relax.

Note: Some things you might want to "get over with": shopping, cooking, homework, a difficult conversation, a visit or phone call that you don't want to make, doing your taxes, etc.

Your Turn

Conduct a survey. Ask three of your classmates the questions below. Take notes in the chart. Then, write sentences about your classmates. Follow the example.

1. First ask, "Are you the type of person who likes to get things over with, or are you the type of person who says, 'Don't do today what you can do tomorrow'?"
2. After you get a response, ask, "Why?"
3. Then ask, "Can you give me an example?"

Classmate 1	**Classmate 2**	**Classmate 3**
_____ likes to get things over with	_____ likes to get things over with	_____ likes to get things over with
_____ doesn't try to get things over with	_____ doesn't try to get things over with	_____ doesn't try to get things over with
Reasons:	Reasons:	Reasons:
Examples:	Examples:	Examples:

Example sentences: *Adam likes to get things over with because he doesn't want to worry about doing them. For example, he does his taxes early.*

5. tálk someone ínto doing something = convince (persuade) someone to do something

ALL CLEAR ?
Yes No

Grammar Note: This expression is followed by a gerund (verb +ING) or the word "it."

A: What are you doing here? I thought you were going to stay home.
B: Lisa **talked me into coming**.

A: You bought a new car?
B: Yup! My wife **talked me into it.**

Opposite: **tálk someone óut of doing something** = convince (persuade) someone *not* to do something

Grammar Note: This expression is also followed by a gerund (verb +ING) or the word "it."

A: I thought you were going away this weekend.
B: I was going to go mountain climbing, but my brother **talked me out of it** because the weather is so bad. (*OR:* . . . my brother **talked me out of going . . .**)

Your Turn

Alice is talking about trying to talk her boyfriend into doing or not doing certain things. Complete her sentences with *talk* ____ *into* and *talk* ____ *out of.* Remember to follow these expressions with gerunds or *it.*

1. Adam doesn't want to go dancing tonight, but I'm going to try to ______________________________.
2. Adam plans to go to college far away, but I want to ______________________________ because I want him to live near me.
3. Adam wants to invite his friends to dinner tonight, but I'm going to try to ______________________________ because I'm tired.
4. Adam isn't planning to buy a car, but I hope I can ______________________________ because I don't like taking the bus.

6. after áll . . . = introduces a good, logical reason or explanation for what someone is saying. This expression is similar to the word *because,* but it is stronger.

Note: This expression often comes after a statement in which someone gives advice with "should." The purpose of adding information after the expression *after all* is to convince/persuade the listener with a reason.

- **Situation:** I know you're busy, but we should go out to dinner.
  Good/Logical reason: After all, your birthday comes only once a year.

Because sentence: I know you're busy, but we should go out to dinner *because* your birthday comes only once a year.

- **Situation**: We should study idioms and other expressions.
  Good/Logical reason: After all, they're very common in English.

Because sentence: We should study idioms and other expressions *because* they're very common in English.

Your Turn

After each sentence, add sentences with *after all.*

1. My boss should give me a raise. **After all**, ______________________________.
2. They should give me a nice birthday present. **After all**, ______________ ______________________________.

7. **háve something in mínd** = have something (a possibility) already in your thoughts

A: I was thinking of getting him a present.
B: What do you **have in mind**?
(= What are you thinking about getting him?)

A: What do you want to get her for her birthday?
B: I **have** two things **in mind**. Can you help me decide?
A: Sure. What are you thinking of?

A: Let's get her a gift certificate for her birthday.
B: That's exactly what I **had in mind**!

8. **gó báck and fórth (between/about)** = keep changing your mind about what to do—this or that

Note: You can physically go back and forth, and you can go back and forth in your mind.

Grammar Note: You can **go back and forth *between*** one thing AND another thing. You can **go back and forth *about*** something.

A: I can't decide where to take my mom to dinner for her birthday. I **go back and forth between** Cafe Blue and Chez Marie.

B: Oh, I think you should take her to Cafe Blue. I just ate there last week and it was fantastic. I'm sure she'd love it.

Note: To emphasize that someone continues to change his or her mind, it is common to say, "I **keep going back and forth.**" Notice that after the verb "keep," you need to use a gerund.

- One minute I think I should pack my bags and move across the country. And the next minute I think I should stay where I am. I **keep going back and forth about** moving!

Your Turn: Listening Challenge

Sam and his wife Ann are retired. They are each trying to make a decision. Listen to them talk about their situations. Then, write sentences with the expression, *go back and forth about.*

1. Sam ____
____.

2. Ann ____
____.

9. **lóok fórward to (something)** = feel good in the present when thinking about something good that will happen in the future

Grammar Notes:

- It is very common to use this expression in the present continuous tense because a person has positive feelings NOW about the future:

  Rosemary and Pat **are looking forward to** their dinner.

- The word **'to'** in this expression is a preposition, not part of an infinitive. If you want to use a verb after *to,* change the verb to a gerund.

  They **are looking forward to having** dinner together.
  (NOT "looking forward to have dinner.")

Negative:

A: What's wrong?
B: I have a big test today and I'**m not looking forward to** it!

10. **be thróugh (with something)** = be finished/done (often with something that you were actively doing)

Grammar Note: If you want to use a verb after **with**, change the verb to a gerund.

A: Can you help me?
B: Sure. I'll **be through** in a second.

- When we'**re through with** our homework, do you want to take a walk?
- After you'**re through with helping** your sister with her homework, can I talk to you?
- After you'**re through helping** your sister with her homework, can I talk to you? (When you use "through" + gerund, the word "with" is optional.)

Note: You can also **be through** in a psychological way:

- I'**m through with** being lazy. I'm going to get a good job!
- She'**s through with** being a piano teacher. She's going to try to become a famous musician.
- He'**s through with** her. They broke up, and now he's looking for another girlfriend.

NEW EXPRESSION COLLECTION

take/ask for/give a rain check	make a difference	after all . . .
be swamped (with)	get something over with	have something in mind
be drowning in	talk someone into/talk out of	go back and forth
be swimming in		look forward to
be up to one's eyeballs (ears) in		be through with

Exercises

(*See page 169 for pronunciation exercises for Lesson 5. Focus: Stress and Intonation Review.*)

1. Mini-Dialogues

1,23

Read the sentences in Column A. Choose the *best* response from Column B. Not all responses can be used.

When checking this exercise in class, perform each mini-dialogue. One student should read an item from Column A, and another student should read the response from Column B.

1A	1B
___ **1.** They're planning to move and I don't want them to go.	**a.** I got my exams over with and I think I did pretty well.
___ **2.** How'd you like to go to a concert tonight?	**b.** Not yet. I keep going back and forth.
___ **3.** You can have the bike for half price.	**c.** Can you think of any way to talk them out of it?
___ **4.** Did you make your decision?	**d.** Really? You talked me into it. I'll take it.
___ **5.** I want to make some changes around here.	**e.** I'd really like to, but can you give me a rain check? I don't feel very well.
___ **6.** Why do you look so happy?	**f.** It makes no difference if you have an accent. What matters is that you speak clearly.
___ **7.** I want to have perfect pronunciation, but it's impossible.	**g.** They're drowning in work.
	h. What do you have in mind?

2A	2B
___ **1.** What are you going to do this weekend?	**a.** So have I. Can I come with you?
___ **2.** I thought you two were going to Brian's house for dinner.	**b.** I sure am!
___ **3.** She told me she volunteers in an after-school homework program because she wants to make a difference.	**c.** It doesn't make a difference.
___ **4.** When I'm through with finals, I'm going to take a little vacation. After all, I've been working really hard for a long time.	**d.** We were, but we had to take a rain check because Connie had to work late.
___ **5.** He's planning to do something big for his parents' anniversary.	**e.** What does he have in mind?
___ **6.** I'm really looking forward to summer after this long, cold winter, aren't you?	**f.** Good for her!
___ **7.** Let's get all this work over with, and then take a long walk.	**g.** Work, work, work. I'm completely swamped.
	h. I'll never get it all over with, but I'll do what I can.

2. Grammar Practice

Follow the directions and complete the sentences.

Directions	Sentences
1. Add a preposition.	a. I can't go out yet. I'm sorry, but I'm swamped _________ work. b. I can't go out yet. I'm sorry, but I'm drowning _________ work. c. He can't go out tonight. He's up _________ his ears _________ work. d. We can go shopping today or tomorrow. It makes no difference _________ me. e. She doesn't want to come with us. How can we talk her _________ coming? f. He was going to quit his job, but we talked him out _________ quitting. g. You said you wanted to make some changes. What do you have _________ mind? h. Help me! I keep going back and forth _________ the blue car and the white one. i. He's been going back and forth_________ marrying her. j. She's really looking forward _________ marrying him. k. When we're through _________ dinner, can you help me with my homework?
2. Add a gerund.	a. Do you think we can talk the teacher into (make) _________________ our next test easy? b. I need to talk my roommate out of _________________ a dog. c. He doesn't know what to do. They offered him the job, but he keeps going back and forth about (take) _________________ it. d. We're really looking forward to _________________ our grandparents when we go back. e. When you're through _________________ the kitchen, can you clean the living room?
3. Make these sentences negative.	a. We were swamped with work, so we couldn't go. → We _________________ swamped with work, so we could go. b. She studied for the test for five hours and it made a difference. She got an A. → She studied for the test for five hours and it _________________ a difference. She still didn't pass. c. I'm so happy that I got my work over with. Now I can go out. → I'm so upset that I _________________ my work over with. Now I can't go out. d. He went back and forth about marrying her. → He _________________ back and forth about marrying her. He knew she was the girl for him. e. I was looking forward to the party. → I _________________ looking forward to the party, but I decided that I had to go.

3. Error Correction

Find the errors and make corrections.

> Remember that 'to' can be part of an infinitive or it can be a preposition.

1. I'm looking forward to see you.
2. When you're through with clean your room, can you clean mine?
3. When they was through with dinner, they watched TV.
4. I didn't know what to do. I kept going back and forth between take four classes and five classes.
5. A: Where should we go on Sunday?

   B: I have two ideas in my mind.
6. They were going to go skiing when the roads were bad, and luckily we talked them out going.
7. He needed to have a serious conversation with his brother, and now he feels better because he got over with.
8. We're sorry we can't come over tonight. Can we take rain check for next Friday?
9. After the hurricane, the city was swamped in donations.
10. It make no difference if you come tomorrow instead of today.

4. Choosing the Idiom

Rosemary and Pat have finished dinner and are having dessert at a nice restaurant. Fill in the blanks with the *best* possible expressions from the list. Pay special attention to how the expressions are used grammatically. You may need to consider verb tenses, subject-verb agreement, pronouns, prepositions, etc. Not all of the expressions can be used. After you finish, practice reading the dialogue aloud.

be drowning	be through with	get __ over with
talk __ into	talk __ out of	after all
have in mind	go back and forth	look forward to

PAT: Well Mom, I told you I have a surprise. Are you ready?

ROSEMARY: I've been waiting all night.

PAT: OK. Well, here it is. I'm quitting my job at the law firm, and I'm going to change careers!

ROSEMARY: What? My goodness, what do you (1) ______________________________?

PAT: You know I (2) ______________________________ in work I don't like. And you know I've never been really happy as a lawyer. So I've decided to go to cooking school.

ROSEMARY: Cooking school? But you already have a great job! How can I (3) ______________________________ ______________________________ doing this?

PAT: You can't. I (4) ______________________________ being a lawyer and I already got into culinary school.

ROSEMARY: How will you pay for it?

PAT: I saved a lot of money.

ROSEMARY: Hmm . . . and I thought you always wanted to be an actor.

PAT: Actually, I thought about acting school. For a while, I kept (5) ______________________________ ______________________________ between culinary school and acting school, but my friend Alex (6) ______________________________ going to culinary school with him.

ROSEMARY: Who's Alex? Your life is a secret, Pat!

PAT: Oh, Alex is a good friend. And he wants to meet you.

ROSEMARY: Well, I (7) ______________________________ meeting him. What does he do?

PAT: He's a lawyer too, and we both want to change our careers.

ROSEMARY: Well Pat. This is a surprise. I'm in shock! But I can't stop you, and I want you to do what makes you happy. (8) ______________________________, you're my one and only daughter!

5. Sentence Writing

Read the paragraphs. Then, write sentences about what you read. In each sentence, use at least one expression from the box. (**Bolded** words and phrases in the story represent where expressions can go.) Sometimes different expressions can be used. Underline the expressions that you use.

Remember to pay attention to grammar details: verb tenses, prepositions, articles, singular and plural nouns, etc.

Hi, everyone! I'm Jerry and I'd like to talk to you about a problem I had. I used to be a workaholic, but don't worry—I'm OK now.

I had my own business, and I did well. In fact, I **had so much work**, I never had any free time. Whenever anyone asked me to go to the movies or out to dinner, I always **asked if we could go another time.**

I always stayed in my office late because I kept saying, well, I'll **do one more thing so I won't have to do it tomorrow**. And I never took a day off. **It didn't matter** if I was sick. I still went to work. And I have to be honest. Every day when I woke up, I really **wanted to get up and go** to the office.

Then one day, my family told me that I needed help. I asked them what **they were thinking of**—a psychiatrist? And they told me that I needed to talk to somebody—not necessarily a psychiatrist—because I didn't have a healthy life. Wow! Was I surprised to hear this! I thought about what they said, and kept **changing my mind about** getting some help. Then my son **convinced me to make** an appointment.

Use a gerund after "keep."

Well, I was lucky to get really good advice. Now I'm **finished with** being a workaholic. I still work, but I spend more time with my family and friends. **I realize now that** they are the most important people in my life.

be through with	get __ over with	ask for a rain check
talk __ into	after all	be swamped with
have in mind	go back and forth	look forward to
make a difference		

Example: *Jerry* **was swamped with** *work that he never had any free time.*

6. Dictation

You will hear the dictation three times. First, just listen. Second, as you listen, write the dictation on a piece of paper. Skip lines. Third, listen again and check what you have written. Then, look at the dictation in Appendix A on page 184.

Key Words: director, company

7. Questions for Discussion and/or Writing

(For more detailed instructions, see Lesson 1, Exercise 7.)

Discussion: You can answer these questions orally in groups or in the Walk and Talk activity in Appendix B on page 189.

Writing: You can write your own answers to these questions, or you can write the responses that you received from students during the *Walk and Talk* activity.

Questions

1. How would you describe yourself when it comes to work? Rate yourself on a scale of 1 to 5.

1	2	3	4	5
I'm lazy.	I'm a little lazy.	I do only what I have to do.	I'm hardworking.	I'm a workaholic.

2. Explain your answer to number 1: (a) Why did you give yourself this rating? (b) Does the amount you work relate to the type of work that you are doing? In other words, how hard do you work on your English? How hard do you work as a student in general? If you have a job, how hard do you work at your job?
3. In the introductory dialogue, Rosemary is talking on the phone and working on her computer at the same time. This is called "multitasking"—doing more than one thing at a time. Are you so busy that you "multi-task"? If yes, give examples of things you do at the same time.
4. "All work and no play makes Jack a dull boy" is a proverb in English. The message is that hard work without time for fun and relaxation is not healthy. What are some proverbs or expressions related to "work" in your native language?
5. Many people in the United States get just two weeks of vacation a year. Some people see this as a reflection of the strong "work ethic" in American culture. How much is work valued in your native country? What is the average number of weeks of vacation that people get per year?

6. What do you think are the effects of "workaholism"? What are some ways to help people with this problem?
7. Imagine that you really want to go away for the weekend with your friend. But your friend doesn't want to go. Are you the kind of person who would try to talk your friend into going, or would you just forget the idea the first time your friend says no? If you would try to talk your friend into going, what would you say?
8. Have you ever tried to talk someone out of getting married, getting divorced, quitting a job, taking a job, quitting school, gambling, going somewhere, etc.? What happened?

8. Role Play or Write a Dialogue

In the cartoon, Rosemary's daughter Pat is working very hard as the chef of her own, very successful restaurant. She finished culinary school five years ago, and has now become a workaholic like her mother. Today, Pat has been working for ten hours without stopping. She never takes time off to rest, and she looks very tired. Her friend, Alex, tries to talk her into going home.

With a partner, write their conversation. Or, role play the situation. Try to use some expressions from this lesson. Refer to or write on the board the New Expression Collection on page 84. Also, try to use other expressions that you know. But don't feel that it is necessary to have an idiom in every sentence.

Possible starting line: *Pat! You need to sit down and take a break!*

9. Word Search

Complete the expressions. Then, find the underlined words in the puzzle. The words can be spelled backwards. They can also be vertical (↕), horizontal (↔), or diagonal (↗) (↖).

1. I'm sorry. I'd love to come on Saturday night, but I can't. Can I ________________ a rain check?

2. It makes no ________________ to me if we stay home instead of going out. I'm tired.

3. I finally ________________ all that work over with. Let's go out and celebrate.

4. Ssh! You need to be quiet. He's in his office and he's ________________ in work.

5. I'm so happy! I ________________ my parents into taking us to the beach!

6. She's a workaholic and he's addicted to his computer. I need to help them. ________________ all, they're my family and I love them.

7. I know you want to look for an exciting career. But tell me, what do you have in ________________?

8. Are you still going back and ________________ about moving to Hollywood?

9. Aren't you looking ________________ to doing this puzzle?

10. When we're ________________ with doing this puzzle, let's take a break, OK?

P B G A G H R L W V D V P D K
N T M N B Y R U O B R Y K R I
A A U B I R T P X I S B X X U
F K A Q T N J B Q N B V J P A
T E N R H B W K D W B F L R S
E Y J N R X C O F G H X L J X
R F M C O K Y V R O O Z V U O
Z D N S U R F M Z D R T H I C
O E L P G F O I U A E W T L E
L K R W H Y P N N M D J A H R
V L X A G T A D O Y F G N R T
M A J P M Z A E P Q F O W S D
J T K G Z Z N A F Q Y I R Z J
R X A E C N E R E F F I D T R
A D A D P H I Y H Y J W R R H

10. Public Speaking

Sit on the Hot Seat

Answer questions from your classmates. See Appendix C on page 193 for sample questions.

Make a Speech

Prepare a five minute speech on one of the following topics. See Appendix D on page 194 for more information.

- Some Proverbs from My Country
- A Workaholic That I Know
- My Job (OR: The Job I Hope to Have)

Note: Search the Internet if you need to get extra information.

Keep an Inventory
Add to:
Expression Clusters—Appendix E
Expression Collections—Appendices F and G

Lesson 6

Guess Who?

Theme: Juggling School, Work, Family

Warm-Up

1. Is it customary in your native culture for someone to stand behind a friend, cover his or her eyes and say, "Guess who?"
2. People greet (say hello to) each other differently in different cultures. Read the list of the different types of greeting behaviors. Then put a check (√) next to the behaviors that are usual in your native culture. Add comments and details if you wish, and share your information with a partner or your class.

Greeting Behaviors	**Usual in your native culture?**	**Comments/Details**
Nodding your head		
Bowing		
Kissing cheeks (once/twice/three or four times)		
Touching cheeks and kissing the air		
Hugging		
Patting an arm or shoulder		
Shaking hands lightly		
Shaking hands strongly		
Shaking hands, but waiting for a woman to offer her hand first		
Shaking hands, but waiting for someone older to offer a hand first		
Direct but not strong eye contact		
Direct and strong eye contact		
Lowered eyes (no eye contact)		
Hands pressed together with the fingers under the chin		
Smiling		
Other:		

Focused Listening

Before You Listen

Where are the two people in the cartoon? What do you think they are saying to each other?

As You Listen

Ⓐ Close your book. Listen to the conversation between Peter and Laura to find the answers to these questions.

What is their relationship?

What are they talking most about?

2,1

Ⓑ Listen again, but this time listen while you read the conversation.

PETER: Guess who?

LAURA: Oh! I can't believe it! I know it's you, Peter! I haven't seen you **in ages.** How are you?

PETER: Pretty good. How about you?

LAURA: Fine. Busy as always. You know me—I'm such a workaholic. Wow! It's really great to see you. I'd love to **catch up on** your news. Do you have time to sit down? Or were you **on your way** out?

PETER: I was leaving, but I can join you for a few minutes.

LAURA: Great! So tell me, how's your family?

PETER: Well, it keeps getting bigger. We have four kids now. All boys.

LAURA: Four boys? I bet they **keep you busy**!

PETER: They sure do. The baby's only a month old, so Jennie's not working right now. And what's new with you and Jim?

LAURA: **Believe it or not**, he's home with the kids!

PETER: You'**re kidding!**

LAURA: No, I'm not. He talked to his boss about working at home, and **it turned out that** his boss thought it was a good idea. I love it because Jim does all the shopping and cleaning, and we save money on childcare.

PETER: **It sounds too good to be true!** Hmm . . . Maybe that's something we should think about doing **down the road.**

LAURA: I'm sure Jennie would love that. But with four kids, I don't know if you'd have time to get any work done.

PETER: Good point . . . Yikes! It's after 1:00. I have to go and spend **the rest of** the day in meetings. I'm really glad I **ran into you**, Laura. Tell Jim I said hi and that I'll call you soon so we can all have dinner.

LAURA: Great idea! And say hi to Jennie and the kids. See you!

Yikes! = *Wow!*

After You Listen

Ⓐ Read the sentences about the conversation. Circle *T* for *true, F* for *false,* or *?* if you don't know.

1.	Peter, Jennie, Laura, and Jim all know each other.	T	F	?
2.	Peter and Laura are both parents.	T	F	?
3.	Jim has time to shop and clean because he doesn't work.	T	F	?
4.	Peter, Laura, and their spouses will *definitely* see each other again soon.	T	F	?
5.	Peter, Jennie, Laura, and Jim are all very busy people.	T	F	?

Ⓑ **Guess the Meanings**

Below is a list of paraphrases of five of the idiomatic expressions in the conversation. On your own or with a partner, try to guess the five. To do this, make sure that what is written below would easily fit in the conversation.

Paraphrase	Idiomatic Expression
1. in a long time	______________________
2. in the future	______________________
3. saw you without planning to see you	______________________
4. You're joking! You're not serious!	______________________
5. we didn't expect it, but the result was that	______________________

Ⓒ Say the conversation in pairs. Then have two students say the conversation in front of the class.

Understanding the New Expressions

Work with Others

If you're working with a partner or in a small group, read the short dialogues and examples for each expression aloud. Also, complete the Your Turn exercises together. For each expression, circle *Yes* or *No* to show if you understand. If you circled *No,* highlight or underline what is unclear, and ask questions for clarification.

Figure It out on Your Own

Read the short dialogues and examples for each expression. Also, complete the Your Turn exercises that don't need partners. Then, for each expression, circle *Yes* or *No* to show if you understand. If you circled *No,* highlight or underline what is still unclear, and ask questions in class for clarification.

1. **in áges** = in a long, long time

Note:

When people have not done something **in ages**, it means that the last time they did something was *a long time ago.* When you use this expression, you are not stating a specific time in the past. If you want to be specific, you can say "in two years" or "since 2005" instead of "in ages."

I HAVEN'T SEEN MY GRANDPARENTS IN AGES.

THE LAST TIME I SAW MY GRANDPARENTS — NOW

2005 — 2007

Grammar Note: Use *in ages* only in negative sentences and with the present perfect tense.

A: How's Tony these days?
B: I don't know. I haven't seen him **in ages**.

Note:

After someone has said, "I haven't seen you in ages," it is common to follow the expression with a question ("How are you?") or a comment ("You look great!").

A: Jim! I haven't seen you **in ages**! How are you?
B: Pretty good. It's great to see you! What's new with you?

Your Turn

On the left side of the chart, put a check (√) next to the people that you haven't seen in ages and things that you haven't done in ages. Then, complete the chart. After you are finished, exchange papers with a partner and write four sentences about him or her.

People that you haven't seen *in ages*	When was the last time you saw him/her/them?	Sentences
√ my great grandfather	5 years ago	I haven't seen my great grandfather in ages.
____ my sister/brother		
____ my grandparents		
____ my parents		
____ my best friend		
____ my cousins		

Things that you haven't done *in ages*	When was the last time you did that?	Sentences
____ gone to the beach		
____ cleaned my room		
____ seen a movie		
____ called an old friend		
____ checked my e-mail		
____ been on vacation		

Example when you write about your partner: Ying hasn't checked her e-mail in ages.

1. ____

2. ____

3. ____

4. ____

Contrast: **for áges** = for a long time

9 a.m.
11 a.m.
WE'VE BEEN SITTING HERE FOR AGES.
WHEN ARE WE GOING TO HAVE A BREAK?

Note: **For ages** shows duration and it means that something lasts or continues for a long time. When you use this expression, you are not giving a specific amount of time. If you want to be specific, you can say "for two hours" or "since 9 o'clock" instead of "for ages."

Grammar Note: You can use *for ages* in both negative and affirmative sentences, with different verb tenses.

- You've been on the phone **for ages**! It's time to get off!
- Sorry we're late. We were in traffic **for ages**. (OR specifically: We were in traffic *for two hours.*)
- I've been studying English **for ages**. (OR: *for three years*). When am I going to be finished?

ALL CLEAR ?
Yes
No

2. **catch úp (on something)** = get information or do something so you are now up-to-date (current), not behind; do something that you have postponed
(past = caught)

Note: You can catch up on the following: *the news* (about the world), *news* (about someone you know personally), *what's new, your homework, sleep, etc.*

A: Hi, Katie. I haven't talked to you in a long time. How's everything?

B: Oh, I've been so busy, you can't imagine! I got a new job and I'm moving next month. But I'm sorry, I can't talk right now. Why don't we meet for coffee so we can **catch up**? I want to know all about you, too.

- I was on vacation for two weeks, and now I have to **catch up on** my mail, my e-mail, my housework, my homework, and everyone's news.
- She's going to see her old friend on Saturday and they're going to **catch up on** what's new.
- When I had the flu, I didn't do any homework. But when I felt better, I **caught up on** everything.

Contrast: **catch úp (with someone)** = come from behind and join or reach someone ahead (in front of) you

A: Where's Eric?

B: He just left to take the dog for a walk. Hurry and maybe you'll **catch up with** him.

- At the beginning of the race, Jon was ahead (in front). But after five minutes, Paul **caught up with** him.

Your Turn

Complete the sentences with forms of *catch up.*

1. Let's meet for coffee soon. I want to _________________ your news.
2. So many things have been happening in your family. I want to _________________ what's new.
3. We talked for two hours and finally _________________ each other's news.
4. There's Annie! Can you run fast enough to _________________ her?

3. be on one's wáy (to)/be on the wáy (to) = be in the process of coming or going somewhere

A: Where are you?

B: I'm {**on my way** / **on the way**} home.

A: Hi. This is Heather. Is Mollie there?

B: No, sorry Heather. She just left. She's {**on her way to** / **on the way to**} your house.

BE ON THE WAY

Contrast:

(1) **be óut of one's wáy/be óut of the wáy** = be in a direction that someone is *not* going

(2) **be in one's wáy/be in the wáy** = be in someone's path so she/he can't easily see something or go somewhere

BE OUT OF THE WAY

A: I can stop at the store before I pick you up.

B: No, don't. The store **is out of your way** and we don't have time.

- I can't see the movie. That tall guy's head **is in my way/ in the way.**

BE IN THE WAY

Your Turn: Listening Challenge

Read the sentences below. Then, listen to the story about Gabriela. After you listen, complete the sentences with *was* or *were* + expressions from the box. Add any other necessary information.

out of his way	on her way
on their way	in the way

Paramedics are the people who do medical work in ambulances.

1. Gabriela fell down when she ______________________________.
2. When they arrived, it was hard for the paramedics to get to Gabriela because so many students were standing around her. The students ______________________________.
3. Gabriela's classmate drove her home even though her apartment ______________________________.
4. Gabriela put her leg on the back seat when they ______________________________.

4. **kéep (someone) búsy (with)** = stay occupied with something to do (housework, errands, seeing friends, taking music lessons, etc.) (**past = kept)**

- I **keep (myself) busy** with my work and my family.
  My work and my family **keep me busy**.
  My work **keeps me** busy.
- She put on a movie to **keep** her daughter **busy** while she cleaned the house. (She put a movie on to **keep her busy**.)
- The babysitter **kept the children busy with** games and music. (She **kept them busy**.)

Your Turn

Ask three classmates, "What keeps you busy these days?" Take short notes and then write three sentences about your classmates.

Follow these examples:

Juliana keeps busy with her five kids.

Juliana's five kids keep her busy.

5. **belíeve it or nót** = It's difficult to believe, but it's true.

Punctuation Note: This expression is followed by a comma.

- **Believe it or not,** we won the lottery!
- They met two weeks ago, and **believe it or not,** they just got married!

Related Expressions: **I don't believe it! I can't believe it! Can you believe it?**

6. **be kídding** = be joking/not be serious

Expressions: You'**re kídding!**/You **múst be kídding!**

A: I quit my job.
B: Really?
A: No, I'**m kidding**. But I'd really like to!

Speaker A	Speaker B	Speaker A
I won the lottery! She has 16 children. He speaks 12 languages. I quit my job.	**You're kidding!** **You must be kidding!**	No, I'm not! I'm serious!

7. **it turned óut (that/to be)** = after expecting something, something else (surprising) happened

Note: Common sentence patterns with this expression are:

what you expected		**surprise**
____________,	but it turned out that	____________. subject + verb
____________,	but it turned out to be	____________. adjective or noun
____________.	But it turned out that/to be	____________.

- They expected twins, but **it turned out that** they had triplets.
- He thought the trip would take only two hours, but **it turned out that** it took four.
- We thought it was going to be expensive, but **it turned out to be** cheap.
- We thought the baby was going to be a boy. But **it turned out to be** a girl.
- I thought I saw an old friend, but **it turned out not to be** her. It was someone who looked like her.

Note: You can use different subjects and verb tenses with *turn out.*

- She didn't do well in school, but she **turned out to be** a great doctor.
- Don't worry. Everything **will turn out** OK.
- You always worry about your speeches, but they always **turn out** fine.

Note: When you ask a question with **turn out**, you are asking about the result or end of something.

- How did the movie **turn out** after I left?
- Did things **turn out** all right?

Your Turn

Complete the sentences with information about yourself. Then, share what you wrote with a partner.

1. When I first came here, I expected ____.

   But it turned out that ____.

2. When I was very young, I ____.

   But I turned out to be ____.

ALL CLEAR ?

8. **(It) sóunds tóo góod to be trúe!** = It's so wonderful, I can't believe it's true.

Note: The situation that you are talking about may be true, or it may not be true. It depends on the situation.

A: They say that they're in heaven. They have great jobs, they live in a beautiful house, their kids are doing well in school, and they travel around the world every summer.

B: Hmm . . . **It sounds too good to be true!**

- His job **sounds too good to be true**. He works six hours a week and makes a ton of money!
- Don't believe what she said. Her story **sounds too good to be true**.

ALL CLEAR ?

9. **dówn the róad** = in the future

- He's studying English now, but he wants to study nursing **down the road**.
- You don't need to buy a house now. Just try to save money. You'll have a chance to buy a house **down the road**.
- I want to live in the city for a few years, but **down the road**, I want to live in the country.
- Save all that information. We don't need it now, but we may need it **down the road**.

Your Turn

Ask three students, "What is something that you're not doing now, but will do **down the road**?"

Then, write three sentences about your classmates. Use these patterns:

(a) *Down the road,* ______________________________.

(b) (name) *(will* or *is going to)* ____________________ *down the road.*

10. **the rést (of)** = the remainder of; whatever is left

- I finished what I want. Do you want **the rest**?
- I did half of my homework. I'll do **the rest** tomorrow.
- I can watch TV after I finish **the rest of** my homework.
- He's the only one who lives here. **The rest of** his family lives far away.
- Let's have six students come to the front of the class. **The rest of** you will be the audience.
- I'm full. Do you want **the rest of** my ice cream?

ALL CLEAR ?
Yes No

11. **run ínto = bump ínto** = meet unexpectedly **(past = ran)**

The emergency number in the United States is 911. What is the emergency number in your native country?

A: I **ran into** our old math teacher in the supermarket. I couldn't believe it.
B: I bet you never expected to **run into** him!

Contrast:

A: Look! That crazy driver **ran into** (= crashed into) a tree.
B: I'm calling 911.

NEW EXPRESSION COLLECTION

in ages	keep busy (with)	it sounds too good to be true
for ages	believe it or not	down the road
catch up	be kidding	the rest of
be/on/in/out of the way	it turned out	run into

Exercises

(See page 171 for pronunciation exercises for Lesson 6 Focus: Thought Groups and Rhythm/Linking.)

1. Mini-Dialogues

2,3

Read the sentences in Column A. Choose the *best* response from Column B. Not all responses can be used.

When checking this exercise in class, perform each mini-dialogue. One student should read an item from Column A, and another student should read the response from Column B.

1A	1B
___ 1. I saw my old girlfriend at the cafe.	a. We bumped into them at the movies last Friday.
___ 2. This movie is terrible. And it's so long!	b. Did you run into her or did you plan to meet?
___ 3. Can you give me a ride home?	c. Sure, no problem. You're on my way.
___ 4. Have you seen Margaret lately?	d. You're right. Let's go. It feels like we've been here for ages.
___ 5. Did you see what happened?	e. No, I haven't seen her in ages.
___ 6. We need to stop at the ATM before the party.	f. No, because people were in my way.
	g. Do we have to? It's out of our way and we'll be late.

2A	2B
___ 1. Did you hear that they won a million dollars?	a. What did the rest of you do?
___ 2. The party was terrible. Only a few people danced.	b. Because I have to keep busy. I'm so nervous about that job. I jump every time the phone rings.
___ 3. Why is he crying?	c. I sure did! I thought it was a joke, but it turned out to be true.
___ 4. Where were you all weekend?	d. Believe it or not, she turned out to be an English teacher!
___ 5. Why are you running around like that?	e. I'm trying to catch up with you.
___ 6. I remember that Angela didn't like studying English. I wonder what she's doing now.	f. I was catching up on my sleep. During the week I had to get up early every day.
	g. Because his girlfriend left him. I told him that this was a good thing, and that down the road he'll find someone else.

2. Grammar Practice

Follow the directions and complete the sentences.

Directions	Sentences
1. Add a preposition.	a. We've been waiting in line ______________ ages. When are they going to open the door to the theater? b. She hasn't visited her parents ______________ ages, and they're not very happy about that. c. I never read the newspaper when I'm on vacation, so now that I'm back, I have to catch up ______________ the news. d. If you hurry, you might be able to catch up ______________ them. They just left. e. His friends are all athletes. Two of them play basketball, four play tennis, and the rest ______________ them play soccer. f. You'll never believe who I ran ______________ in the store! g. Could you please move your backpack? It's ______________ my way. h. Can you pick up some milk ______________ your way home? i. The road was closed, so we had to drive ten miles out ______________ our way to get to the highway. j. We keep busy ______________ school work and our friends.
2. Add an object pronoun (*me/you/him/her/it/us/them*).	a. Our teacher really keeps ______________ busy with all that homework, doesn't she? b. I'm glad I caught up with ______________. I need to talk to you. c. I don't want to go to the cafeteria because I don't want to run into ______________. d. We all have a lot to do before the party. Why don't you clean the living room, and the rest of ______________ can clean the kitchen?
3. Add an irregular past tense verb.	a. When they were on the plane, they ______________ their kids busy with some special toys and books. b. One Sunday, he ______________ up on a lot of reading. c. We ______________ into our math teacher on the bus.

3. Error Correction

Find the errors and make corrections.

1. I think I lost my cell phone when I was in my way to class.
2. All that homework keep me busy.
3. Toys keep busy the children.
4. I like history, but the rest my family loves science.
5. Don't worry. Nothing bad happened. I kidding.
6. She didn't visit him in ages.
7. We expected the test to be hard, but it turned out being easy.

8. I waited for you in ages, but then I left. I didn't know what to do.

9. When she described her job, her friend said, "It sound too good to be true."

10. Down the road, I'm sure you are a big success.

4. Choosing the Idiom

Sue and Martin are talking at a restaurant. Fill in the blanks with the *best* possible expressions from the list. Pay special attention to how the expressions are used grammatically. You may need to consider verb tenses, subject-verb agreement, pronouns, prepositions, etc. Not all of the expressions can be used. After you finish, practice reading the dialogue aloud.

in ages	run into
on the way	catch up on
you're kidding	believe it or not
for ages	in the way
the rest of	

SUE: Mmmm. I know what I'm getting.

MARTIN: What?

SUE: A hamburger. I haven't had a hamburger (1) ______________________.

MARTIN: I know. You don't eat meat anymore. Remember?

SUE: Well, (2) ______________________, tonight I'm having meat.

MARTIN: (3) ______________________, right?

SUE: No, I'm serious. And I'm ready to order. Where's the waiter? We've been here (4) ______________________.

MARTIN: No, we haven't. We've been here for less than five minutes. And this is a busy place. Relax.

SUE: Hey, Martin! Look over there! Isn't that our English teacher?

MARTIN: Where?

SUE: At that table against the wall.

MARTIN: I can't see. The pole is (5) ______________________.

SUE: Well, I'm sure that's her. I've never (6) ______________________ her outside of school before, have you?

MARTIN: No, never.

SUE: Should we say hello?

MARTIN:	No, we should stay here. I want to (7) ______________ your news. We haven't talked in a long time.
SUE:	Yeah, right. Since yesterday!
MARTIN:	Come on, Sue. It's time for us to have a serious conversation.
SUE:	OK, my friend. But let's relax and have dinner first. We'll have (8) ______________ the evening to talk.

5. Sentence Writing

This time, in this exercise, you will not write *about* the person in the paragraphs. Instead, you will just rewrite the paragraphs with expressions from the box. (**Bolded** words and phrases in the story represent where expressions can go.) Underline the expressions that you use.

Remember to pay attention to grammar details: verb tenses, prepositions, articles, singular and plural nouns, etc.

Hi! You know me. I'm Sue. I know we haven't talked **in a long time** and **you said that you want to know my news**. Well, **you'll probably find this hard to believe**, but I'm not a vegetarian anymore. I know you think **I'm joking**, but I'm not. Maybe I'll change again **in the future**. Who knows?

Well anyway, I'm sure you want to know **all of my other** news. Listen to this! When I was at a restaurant with my friend Martin last week, I thought I saw our English teacher. I was scared, but I went over to her table to say hello. When I got there, **I saw a woman who looked like my teacher, but wasn't.** I was really embarrassed, as you can imagine.

There isn't much else to talk about. I **fill my time** with schoolwork and my part-time job. And I'm applying to college.

I know I've been talking to you **for a long time** and you need to go. Thanks for listening!

it turned out that	be kidding	in ages	catch up on
believe it or not	it turned out not to be	the rest of	for ages
keep busy with	down the road		

Start with: *Hi! You know me. I'm Sue. I know we haven't talked* ***in ages*** *. . .*

6. Dictation

You will hear the dictation three times. First, just listen. Second, as you listen, write the dictation on a piece of paper. Skip lines. Third, look at Appendix A on page 184 to check what you have written.

2,5

7. Questions for Discussion and/or Writing

(For more detailed instructions, see Lesson 1, Exercise 7.)

Discussion: You can answer these questions orally in groups or in the *Walk and Talk* activity in Appendix B on page 190.

Writing: You can write your own answers to these questions, or you can write the responses that you received from students during the *Walk and Talk* activity.

Questions

1. Imagine that you are at a party. You are talking to someone you haven't seen in ages. What kinds of questions do you ask? What topics do you talk about?
2. Imagine that you are at a party. You are talking to someone you don't know, so you need to "make small talk." You talk about the party and the food, and maybe the weather. What else can you talk about? And how can you show that you are listening to the other person?
3. In the introductory dialogue, Peter says that his wife is home (and not at work) because she recently had a baby. Perhaps she is "on maternity leave." In your native country, is it common for women to "get maternity leave" from their jobs? If yes, for how long? Do men get "paternity leave"?
4. In the introductory dialogue, Laura says that her husband works at home and takes care of the shopping and cleaning. Some people might call him a "househusband." What do you think of this idea? Why?
5. What is something that you haven't done in ages that you would like to do again?
6. What is something that you have been doing for ages that you would like to stop doing?
7. What are your plans for after class? In other words, what do you plan to do for the rest of the day or evening?

8. Role Play

In the cartoon, old classmates are catching up on each other's news at a reunion. Imagine that it is ten years from now, and that the reunion is for your current English class. In other words, you and your classmates are in the picture.

In your role play, you will meet and greet at least three different classmates. Try to use some expressions from this lesson. Refer to or write on the board the New Expression Collection on page 106. Also, try to use other expressions that you know. But don't feel that it is necessary to have an idiom in every sentence.

To get started, you should warm up by having one conversation with a partner. Then, everyone should get up and walk around the classroom as you meet and greet your "old" classmates. Remember, this conversation is taking place ten years from now, so use your imagination.

Possible starting lines:
(Name), I haven't seen you in ages! How are you?
(Then, ask for news about families and jobs, etc.)

Possible ending lines: *It was nice talking to you.* OR
It was great seeing you.

9. Tic-Tac-Toe

Directions

a. Your teacher will put tic-tac-toe lines on the board, with expressions in the nine spaces.

b. The class should be divided into two teams, *X* and *O*. Flip a coin (choose "heads or tails") to see which team goes first.

c. To get an *X* or an *O* in a space, a team has to make a sentence with the expression in that space. The sentence should be correct in grammar and meaning. (Sometimes it will be necessary to create two sentences to create a context for an item.) Team members can plan what they will say for up to 30 seconds. Students should take turns giving the answers.

d. The first team to get three *X*'s or *O*'s in a straight line wins. The line can be horizontal (↔), vertical (↕), or diagonal (↗ ↖).

e. When you finish a game, if there are any expressions that are not covered by *X*'s or *O*'s, you can keep them for another game. You can add other expressions to the spaces already used and play again.

for ages	**in ages**	**too good to be true**
it turned out that	**it turned out to be**	**down the road**
bump into	**catch up with**	**the rest of**

Culture Note

The *real* Tic-Tac-Toe is a "paper and pencil" game with two players, X and O. The winner gets three Xs or Os in a horizontal, vertical, or diagonal line. Do you play this game in your native country?

10. Public Speaking

Sit on the Hot Seat

Answer questions from your classmates. See Appendix C on page 193 for sample questions.

Make a Speech

Prepare a five minute speech on one of the following topics. See Appendix D on page 194 for more information.

- How I (or my parents) juggle school/work/kids
- Nonverbal behavior in my native country (gestures, facial expressions, distance between people)
- My experience at a school reunion
- The advantages and disadvantages of being a housewife or househusband
- Maternity leave policies in different countries
- The history of Tic-Tac-Toe

Note: Search the Internet if you need to get extra information.

Keep an Inventory
Add to:
Expression Clusters—Appendix E
Expression Collections—Appendices F and G

Review — Lessons 5 and 6

Collocation Match-Up

Collocations are special combinations of words that can be idioms or other phrases and expressions. Find collocations from *Lessons 5* and *6* by matching the words from Column A with words in Column B. (You will probably be able to make additional expressions that are not from Lessons 5 and 6. Put these in the box.)

A		B
1. swamped	____________	over with
2. drowning	____________	ages
3. please give me	____________	or not
4. it makes no difference	____________	of the day
5. she talked us	____________	working in the garden
6. that's what	____________	me into cooking
7. for	____________	where we go
8. it turned out	____________	forth
9. down	____________	way
10. caught	____________	to relaxing
11. be through with	____________	with work
12. run	____________	in work
13. let's get this	____________	busy
14. the rest	____________	I had in mind
15. go back and	____________	the road
16. in my	____________	a rain check
17. look forward	____________	into them
18. he talked	____________	into driving
19. they keep me	____________	to be great
20. believe it	____________	up with old friends

Additional Collocations

Review — Lessons 5 and 6

Crossword Puzzle

Across

4 It sounds too good to be ___, but I talked them into helping us.

5 I'll wash the dishes. ___ all, you cooked.

6 We're really looking forward to ___ on vacation.

9 It makes no ___ to me what time we leave.

11 We talked them into ___ us 500 miles in their new car!

13 I have no idea what to get them. What do you have in ___?

Down

1 When our flight was delayed, we ___ busy playing cards.

2 It ___ out that they weren't kidding.

3 You're always ___ with things to do. Take a break!

7 ___ it or not, I just bumped into them!

8 We finally ___ up with each other while we were on the train to the city.

10 We've been waiting for the bus ___ ages.

12 Down the ___, when I'm through with school, I'm going to start a business.

How are you doing? Complete the Self-Evaluation Questionnaire in Appendix H on page 203. Use the Study Tips in Appendix I on page 204.

Lesson 7

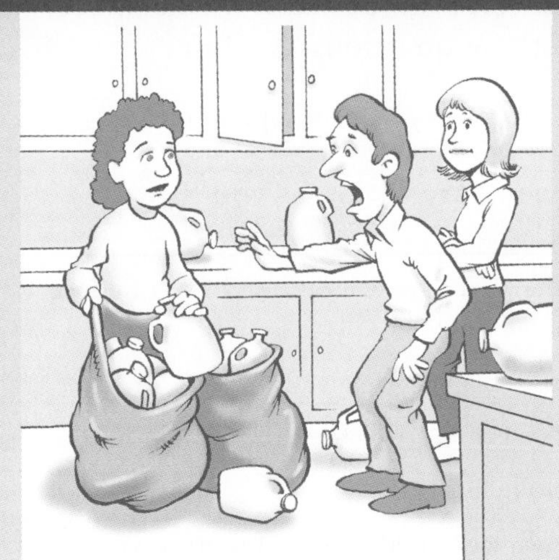

Don't Throw It Away—Recycle!

Theme: Taking Care of the Environment

Warm-Up

Is there a recycling program in your neighborhood? If you throw bottles, cans, and newspapers away in the regular garbage, do you ever think about the environment?

Focused Listening

Before You Listen

Look at the cartoon. Michael, Lee, and Kathy are cleaning up after a big event. Michael is talking to Kathy. What do you think he is saying to her?

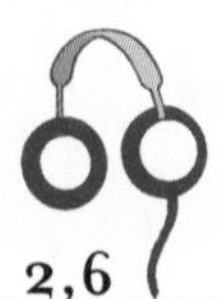

As You Listen

(A) Close your book. Listen to the conversation between Michael, Lee, and Kathy to find the answers to these questions.

What's the problem? How do they solve the problem?

(B) Listen again, but this time read the conversation as you listen.

MICHAEL:	**Hold it**, Kathy! **What in the world** are you doing? **I can't believe my eyes!**
KATHY:	What's the problem?
MICHAEL:	Well, don't you recycle? How can you **throw** glass **away**?
KATHY:	Michael! I was only trying to help . . .
MICHAEL:	I know, I know. But I'm really surprised, Kathy. I thought you **cared about** the environment and . . .
KATHY:	I *do* care, but there's no place to recycle bottles here, and I wanted to help **clean up**. You make me **feel** so **guilty**.
MICHAEL:	I'm sorry. I did go a little crazy. It's just that recently I **did** some **research on** pollution and **found out** that we'**re running out of** places to put our garbage.
LEE:	Listen you two, why don't we all **go through** these bags and **take** the bottles **out**. I'll take them home and recycle them.
MICHAEL:	Oh Lee, you don't have to take them all. Why don't we each take a few?
KATHY:	Yeah, good idea Mike! Well, let's get started so we can all go home.

After You Listen

(A) Read the sentences about the conversation. Circle *T* for *true*, *F* for *false*, or *?* if you don't know.

1. Kathy doesn't care about the environment. T F ?
2. Lee provides a solution to the problem. T F ?
3. Michael wants to become a politician. T F ?
4. They are all unhappy because everyone else left early and they have to clean up. T F ?
5. Lee is going to take all the bottles home. T F ?

(B) Guess the Meanings

Below is a list of paraphrases of five of the idiomatic expressions in the conversation. On your own or with a partner, try to guess the five. To do this, make sure that what is written below would easily fit in the conversation.

Paraphrase	Idiomatic Expression
1. look inside and search	______________________
2. discovered	______________________
3. remove	______________________
4. were concerned about	______________________
5. stop	______________________

(C) Say the conversation in groups of three. Then, have three students say the conversation in front of the class.

Understanding the New Expressions

Work with Others

If you're working with a partner or in a small group, read the short dialogues and examples for each expression aloud. Also, complete the Your Turn exercises together. For each expression, circle *Yes* or *No* to show if you understand. If you circled *No,* highlight or underline what is unclear, and ask questions for clarification.

Figure It out on Your Own

Read the short dialogues and examples for each expression. Also, complete the Your Turn exercises that don't need partners. Then, for each expression, circle *Yes* or *No* to show if you understand. If you circled *No,* highlight or underline what is still unclear, and ask questions in class for clarification.

1. **Hóld it!** = Wait! Stop!

A: Wait! **Hold it** for a second. I have to move my hand.
B: Are you OK now?
A: Yeah, I'm ready. OK. Slowly now . . .

- Hey, you guys. **Hold it!** We're coming, too.

Note: This expression does not mean that someone is holding something. We often say "Hold it!" in an urgent situation to ask someone to stop or wait.

2. **Whát in the wórld? = Whát on éarth?** = What? (with real surprise/shock) You can express surprise this way with people you are close to, such as friends and family members.

A: **What in the world** are you doing here?
B: I came to surprise you on your birthday.

Note: The question words *who, what, when, where, why,* and *how* can all be used in a similar way to show different strong feelings. Notice the different verb tenses in the questions in the chart.

Questions	Feelings Expressed
1. Who on earth is calling us at 4:00 A.M.?	surprise, anger, disbelief, fear
2. What in the world are you wearing?	surprise
3. When on earth will they get here?	impatience, concern (worry), anger
4. Where in the world have you been?	anger, relief that someone is safe
5. Why on earth did they try to drive in this weather?	concern, criticism
6. How in the world can we get there by 8:00? It's already 7:30!	concern, impatience

Your Turn

Imagine that you and your partner are having an emotional conversation. Together, express your emotions in the following questions. (Possible topics to be talking about: *how hard English is; a crazy thing that just happened; worry about something that you need to do.*)

1. Who in the world ______________________________?
2. What on earth ______________________________?
3. When in the world ______________________________?
4. Where on earth ______________________________?
5. Why in the world ______________________________?
6. How on earth ______________________________?

3. **I cán't belíeve my éyes!** = I can't believe what I see because I am very surprised. **(past = couldn't)**

A: **I can't believe my eyes!** Why did you dye your hair blond?
B: Relax. It's just a wig.

Similar expression: **I cán't beliéve my éars!** = I can't believe what I hear because I am very surprised.

A: **I can't believe my ears!** Six months ago, you couldn't speak a word of English. You've certainly learned a lot!
B: Thanks. I study a lot, and my roommate helps me.

4. **throw something awáy = throw something óut** = put in the garbage (trash) = **toss** (informal) **(past = threw)**

A: Ugh! Smell this cheese.
B: It must be two months old. **Throw it away! (Toss it!)**

A: Where are my old jeans?
B: I **threw them out.**

Pronunciation Note: "Threw" is pronounced exactly like "through." Be sure to put the front of your tongue between your teeth and blow air to produce the *th* sound. If your tongue is behind your teeth, you will be saying a different word, "true."

Contrast: **gét ríd of (something)** = take some action so you won't have something anymore. You can put something in the garbage or give something to a person or place that needs what you don't want.

A: I know that you want to **get rid of** those old clothes, but don't **throw** them **away**. Donate them to a homeless shelter.
B: That's a great idea.

Culture Note

In the United States, many people use things that are "used." People often give children's clothes and toys to friends and relatives with younger children. Some people buy clothes at secondhand stores. And it is common to donate used items to help the poor. In your native country, is it the same or different?

Your Turn

Think about things that you own but should get rid of. List three of these things in the chart, and put a check (√) in the appropriate column to indicate where each item should go. Then, write a sentence about each item. Share your sentences with a partner.

Things you own	Throw away?	Give away to friends/family?	Donate?
1.			
2.			
3.			

Example: *I should throw away my old jeans.*

1. ______________________________
2. ______________________________
3. ______________________________

5. **cáre about (someone** or **something)** = have an interest in and be concerned about someone or something; when you *care about* something, you feel the care in your heart

Care about people:

A: He **cares about** his family, but he wants to leave home and get his own apartment.
B: So what's the problem?
A: His family doesn't want him to move.

A: Why didn't you give him some money? Don't you **care about** the homeless?
B: Sure I do. But I don't like giving money on the street.

Care about an idea:

A: Do you **care about** politics? the environment? money?
B: No. I don't **care about** all that. I just **care about** music.

Contrast: **táke cáre (of)**

(1) Perform actions (such as feeding and bathing a baby) because it is your responsibility to do that.

- They (don't) **take** good **care of** their children.
  their elderly parents.
  their house.

- You need to **take care of** yourself. Eat better and sleep more!

(2) Babysitters can be asked to **take care of** or **look after** a baby for a few hours.

A: Can you **take care of (look after)** the baby for a few hours so we can go to a movie?
B: I'd be glad to. You go have a good time and don't worry about us.

(3) **Take care of** can also mean *fix* something or *solve a problem*.

A: My car won't start and I don't know what to do.
B: Take it easy. I'll **take care of** it.

- I had a problem at the bank, but luckily someone **took care of** it.

Your Turn

Complete the chart. Then, write sentences about who and what you *care about* and *take care of.* Share your sentences with a partner.

Two people I care about	Two things I care about	Two people and/or things I take care of
1.		
2.		

6. clean úp (something) = clean *completely* after a specific event, such as a party

- That was a great party. Do you think we should **clean up** now, or do it tomorrow morning?
- OK kids. It's time to **clean up** your toys. It's almost bedtime!

A: Did you have any damage from the storm?
B: Yes, we had some water damage. And some broken windows. It took us two weeks to **clean up**.

Contrast: **to cléan** = make clean, usually on a regular basis

A: We **clean** (vacuum, dust, wash the kitchen and bathroom floor) every Saturday morning.
B: *Every week?* We **clean** only once a month!

7. **féel gúilty (about)** = feel that something bad that happened was your responsibility **(past = felt)**

Note: Use a noun or gerund after the preposition *about*.

A: Uh-oh! You sound like you have a cold, too.
B: Yeah, I'm really sick.
A: You probably got it from me. I'm sorry. I **feel guilty (about giving** it to you).

- When my parents told me that I don't e-mail or call them enough, I **felt guilty**.
- When my dog stole my socks, he **didn't feel guilty**.

Contrast: **be gúilty (of)** = be the one who did something wrong, often in a legal sense ≠ **be ínnocent (of)**

- She'**s guilty of** murder, but you can see from her face that she doesn't **feel guilty**.
- She said she **was innocent**, but she'**s guilty**.

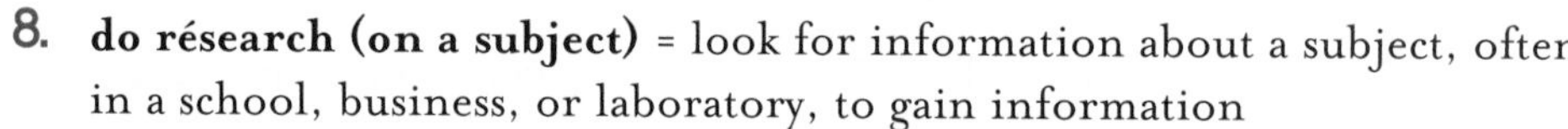

8. **do résearch (on a subject)** = look for information about a subject, often in a school, business, or laboratory, to gain information

Note: Possible ways you can do research—by reading print material or material online, asking people questions in surveys, and by doing experiments in a laboratory

Grammar Note: "Research" is a noncount noun. It is incorrect to make it plural and say "researches."

A: Where's Tony?
B: Oh, he's home at his computer. He can't come with us because he's working on his research paper.
A: That's too bad. Do you know what his topic is?
B: I think he'**s doing research on** water pollution.

A: Excuse me. We're **doing research on** language learning. Can we ask you a few questions about your experience learning English?
B: Sure.

- When he was in high school, he **didn't do** much **research**, but now in college, he's **doing** a lot of **research**.
- She wants to **do research on** diseases that people have when they're old.

9. **find óut** = discover/get information **(past = found)**

A: Where's Larry?
B: I don't know. Don't worry. I'**ll find out** where he is.

Contrast: **find** = locate someone or something that you can *see*. (Generally, when you "find" information, you can see it—in a book, on a Web site, etc.)

ALL CLEAR ? Yes No

find someone or something	find out information
I found Sam in the bookstore. I can't find my keys. I found the (written) information on the Web.	Let's find out where Sam went. I need to find out where my keys are.

Note: **Find out** can be followed by many different patterns of words. Some of the patterns are below.

find out + *who* + verb *Note:* These are statements, not questions. Use a period.	I need to **find out** *who* is doing research on John Kennedy. Let's **find out** *who* wants to come with us.
find out + *what, where, when, what time, why, how, how much, if, that* + subject + verb *Note:* These are statements, not questions. Use a period. Pay attention to the order of words. Question: How is he? Statement: Let's find out *how* he is.	We **found out** *what* she wants for her birthday. We need to **find out** *where* the information desk is. Let's **find out** *when* the movie starts. Let's **find out** *what* time the movie starts. I didn't **find out** *why* they did that. I'll **find out** *how* he is. They can't buy that until they **find out** *how much* it costs. Can you **find out** *if* I can get an appointment? When they **found out** *that* he was in the hospital, they called right away.
find out + *what, where, when, how, how much* + infinitive *Note:* Using the infinitive in these sentences gives the meaning of "should"—*I need to find out what to do. = I need to find out what I should do.*	I need to **find out** *what* to do. *where* to go. *when* to call. *how* to fix it. *how much* to get.
find out + *about* + noun or gerund *Note:* Think about activities when you use gerunds.	We need to **find out** more *about* air pollution. We need to **find out** *about* it. Let's **find out** *about* sailing in the bay/renting a house/getting a loan.

Your Turn: Listening Challenge

Listen to Alice and Mark, who are students. Then, complete the chart.

Alice	• found	• found out about • needs to find out about
Mark	• found	• found out what he doesn't want to • found out that he doesn't want to • found out that he wants to

10. **run óut (of)** = have no more of something, such as milk, time, gas **(past = ran)**

- We'**re running out of** milk. Can you go to the store?
- Sorry everyone. We **ran out of** time. We'll finish this tomorrow.

A: Where are you going?

B: To that gas station over there. I don't think there'll be another station for miles and miles, and I don't want to **run out of** gas.

11. **go thróugh (something)** = search/look for something that is mixed with other things; look at a collection of things so that you can take out what you want or don't want anymore.

A: I can't find my paycheck.
B: Did you look in your wallet?
A: Three times. I **went through** everything, but my check wasn't there.

A: Look at this! When I was cleaning, I was **going through** some old photos and found this baby picture.
B: That's you? I can't believe it. You were really cute.

Note: Some things that police might go through when they are searching for something are houses, cars, files, etc. Some things that you might go through when you are cleaning are old clothes, old school notes and books. And to review school work, you can go through your notes and tests.

Contrast: **go thróugh** = experience a difficult time psychologically

- Many families are **going through** hard times because of unemployment.
- They **went through** a difficult divorce.

12. **take something óut (of)** = remove something from an enclosed area

Grammar Note: When you use a prepositional phrase with 'of' after *take out,* always put the object between *take* and *out.*

take out	**take out *of***
Take out the juice./ Take the juice out.	Take *the juice* out of the refrigerator. [Incorrect: Take out of the refrigerator the juice.]

A: Hurry up! **Take** the letter **out of** the envelope! I can't wait!
B: Calm down. I'**ll take** it **out**.

A: Where are my keys? They were in my pocket a minute ago.
B: Are you sure? I think I saw you **take them out** and put them on the counter. *OR*
I think I saw you **take them out of** your pocket and put them on the counter.

Note: You take something **out** of an enclosed area such as a bag or an envelope. You take something **off** a surface or a space that is not enclosed, such as a table.

She **took** her coat **out of** the closet.
She **took** her plate **off** the table.

Your Turn

Complete the chart. Then, write sentences. Follow the examples. Share your sentences with a partner.

You can take things out of:	**What can you take out?**
a closet	pants
______	______
______	______

You can take things off:	**What can you take off?**
a table	plates
______	______
______	______

Example sentences: She took her pants out of the closet.
He took the plates off the table.

NEW EXPRESSION COLLECTION

hold it	get rid of	do research
What in the world?	care about	find out
What on earth?	take care of	run out of
I can't believe my eyes/ears!	clean up	go through
throw away/throw out	feel guilty about	take something out of

Exercises

*(See page 175 for pronunciation exercises for Lesson 7. Focus: Voiced and Voiceless Consonants and the -*ed *Ending.)*

1. Mini-Dialogues

Read the sentences in Column A. Choose the *best* response from Column B. Not all responses can be used.

When checking this exercise in class, perform each mini-dialogue. One student should read an item from Column A, and another student should read the response from Column B.

1A	1B
___ 1. Hold it! Wait for me!	a. My pet snake.
___ 2. I care about learning English, but sometimes I get a little lazy.	b. Well, if you feel that way, why don't you ride your bike?
___ 3. OK, kids. It's time to clean up. Put everything away where you found it.	c. Uh-oh—I threw it out. Was it important?
___ 4. When should I take the cake out of the oven?	d. Do you want to come with us?
___ 5. Oh no! My pen just ran out of ink.	e. Here's an extra. You can use it.
___ 6. What in the world is that?	f. I know what you mean. It's hard work.
___ 7. Where's the bag that was on the table?	g. Get rid of them.
___ 8. I feel guilty about driving. It adds to the air pollution around here.	h. Where should I put the paint?
	i. I don't know. Let me find out.

2A	2B
___ 1. I lost my ring. I'm going to go through everything in my room till I find it.	a. Yup, it's me! Surprise!
___ 2. What on earth happened here?	b. Never.
___ 3. How's work?	c. I'm sorry I can't. My mom had surgery and I'm taking care of her.
___ 4. Jim? Is that you? I can't believe my eyes!	d. I can't believe my ears!
___ 5. OK. It's time for your test. Take everything off your desks.	e. Everything? Good luck!
___ 6. Can you come over tonight?	f. I found it on the Internet.
___ 7. When are you going to get rid of those old jeans?	g. Pretty interesting. I'm doing research on climate change.
___ 8. Did you hear? The jury said she's innocent! She's getting out of jail this afternoon!	h. Well, I was on the phone while the kids were playing and I didn't notice that they were taking everything out of the drawers.
	i. Everything? Can't we use our dictionaries?

2. Grammar Practice

Follow the directions and complete the sentences.

Directions	Sentences
1. Add a preposition.	a. He took the dishes out __________ the cabinet. b. She didn't take the cookbook __________ the shelf. c. I need to go __________ my binder and organize all of my handouts. d. We ran out __________ cereal so we went out for breakfast. e. I want to do research __________ chimpanzees. f. I used to feel guilty __________ not working harder. g. Don't you care __________ your future? h. Take care __________ your health! i. What __________ the world am I going to do? j. What __________ earth are you saying? k. Let's get rid __________ all that junk in the garage. l. Can you look __________ my kids for an hour?
2. Add a gerund.	a. I care a lot about __________ English. b. Let's find out about __________ on a tour of the city. c. He felt guilty about __________ three pieces of chocolate cake.
3. Add a past tense verb.	a. After we __________ through all of our old cassettes, we decided that we didn't want to keep any. So we __________ them all away. b. When we were finished with dinner, he __________ out his wallet and paid for everyone. c. When we went shopping, we __________ out of cash, so we had to use a credit card. d. When I __________ out that she __________ all that research on our ancestors, I __________ guilty that I didn't help her. e. When I saw them after ten years, I __________ believe my eyes. f. After the flood, we __________ rid of a lot of our furniture.

3. Error Correction

Find the errors and make corrections.

1. I did a lot of researches when I was a student.
2. They're very busy because they take care their children and their elderly parents.
3. Every Saturday, I clean up.
4. After the party, I cleaned.
5. We found out a good article in the newspaper.
6. What in earth is going on here?

7. I need to find out where is he going.
8. He has a lot of old clothes and he wants to throw away them.
9. They fell guilty because they forgot my birthday.
10. She took out of her closet all of her clothes.

4. Choosing the Idiom

Anita and Philip are watching the news. They are talking about an oil spill. Fill in the blanks with the best possible expressions from the list. Pay special attention to how the expressions are used grammatically. You may need to consider verb tenses, subject-verb agreement, pronouns, etc. After you finish, practice reading the dialogue aloud.

go through
what in the world
find out about
feel guilty
run out of
care about
can't believe my eye
throw away
take care of

ANITA: (1) ______________________________ is happening to the earth? I (2) __________________________!

PHILIP: What happened?

ANITA: There was another oil spill. There's oil covering miles of the ocean near the coast.

PHILIP: Again?

ANITA: Yes, again. What kind of world will our children live in? The forests are being cut down, we have air and water pollution, we

(3) __________________________ too much and don't recycle enough.

And now we (4) __________________________ places for our garbage.

We need to (5) __________________________ the earth, don't you think?

PHILIP: Yes, you're absolutely right. But if you (6) __________________________ the earth so much, why don't you do something about it?

ANITA: Are you trying to make me (7) __________________________ , Philip?

PHILIP: No, I'm not. I just think you should (8) __________________________ ways you can help. You're passionate about this—you really care. I think you should think about becoming a politician!

5. Sentence Writing

Read the paragraphs. Then, write sentences about what you read. In each sentence, use at least one expression from the box. (**Bolded** words and phrases in the story represent where expressions can go.) Underline the expressions that you use.

Remember to pay attention to grammar details: verb tenses, prepositions, articles, singular and plural nouns, etc.

Hi! I'm Mike. Do you want to know what I'm doing? Well, it's April, and it's time for spring cleaning. To be honest, this is the first time in five years that I'm completely cleaning my room, so you can imagine that I have a lot of stuff **to put in the garbage**. But I'm going to give some stuff away, too. (If it's not in bad condition, of course.)

When I looked in my closet, **I felt bad about** all the money I wasted on clothes that I never wear. Actually, while **I was looking at all my shirts one by one**, I did find one or two that I really like, so that was good. The truth is, when **I removed them from** my closet, I was surprised because I didn't remember buying them!

Oh—I should tell you—a few hours ago my mom came into my room. You should have seen the look on her face! She **couldn't believe what she saw**, and I can understand that. But she told me that she's glad I'm finally **getting things out of here—putting them in the garbage** or donating them. She also told me that I have to stop throwing my clothes on the floor and **put them where they belong.**

The good news is that when I'm finished here, we're going to celebrate by going out to dinner. That was good news—because you know that I'm working so hard that I'm getting really hungry.

But I'm not done. I have to **look on the Internet for local places** where I can take my donations. I have to get back to work right now. See you later!

feel guilty about	throw away	go through	X couldn't believe __ eyes
take care of	get rid of	take out of	find out where

Example: *Mike has a lot of stuff to* ***throw away****.*

6. Dictation

You will hear the dictation three times. First, just listen. Second, as you listen, write the dictation on a piece of paper. Skip lines. Third, look at Appendix A on page 184 to check what you have written.

2,10

Key Words: suddenly, recycling, environment, suggested

7. Questions for Discussion and/or Writing

(For more detailed instructions, see Lesson 1, Exercise 7.)

Discussion: You can answer these questions orally in groups or in the *Walk and Talk* activity in Appendix B on page 191.

Writing: You can write your own answers to these questions, or you can write the responses that you received from students during the *Walk and Talk* activity.

Questions

1. What do you do to help take care of the earth? Do you: recycle, avoid throwing garbage out of car windows, avoid littering? What other things can you and other people do?
2. Are there recycling programs in your native country? If yes, what kinds of things are recycled? Explain how the recycling system works.
3. Think of special things that you own and will *never* get rid of. These are things with "sentimental value." What are these things and why do you want to keep them forever?
4. What do you usually do to get rid of things you don't use anymore? Do you donate them to an organization? Do you give them to friends? Do you throw them away? Explain.
5. If you had to do a research project, what would your topic be? Why?
6. When you are invited to dinner at someone's house, do you offer to help clean up? Why or why not?
7. What is one thing that you care a lot about? What is one thing that you don't care about at all?
8. Imagine that some new students are coming to your English program. What do they need to find out about before classes start?

8. Role Play or Write a Dialogue

In the cartoon, Anita and Philip are in a crowded high school gym. They and their neighbors are there because of a train derailment (a train went off its tracks). The train was carrying a dangerous chemical and everyone had to leave the area.

Anita, Philip, and their neighbors will have to stay in the gym for at least one night while government officials and scientists try to find out how dangerous the situation is and what needs to be done.

With a partner, role play or write a conversation between Anita and Philip. If you role play this situation, you might want to include some of the neighbors. Try to use some expressions from this lesson. Refer to or write on the board the New Expression Collection on page 128. Also, try to use other expressions that you know. But don't feel that it is necessary to have an idiom in every sentence.

Possible starting line: *I can't believe that this happened to us!*

9. Unscramble and Find the Secret Message

Unscramble the words to make sentences with the expressions from this lesson. Then, find the secret message at the bottom of the page.

TAHW ON HEATR REA OUY OINDG

?

11

I NAC'T VIBLEEE YM AERS

' !

42 17 43 53 3 52 35

EHS DUONF UTO OHW NLEEADC PU

.

7 56

EW ARN OTU OF IETM

.

44 4 55

TLE'S GO UGROHTH HET SETT GNIAA

' .

25 9

EH OKTO HER CRUTPEI TUO OF SIH ELWALT

.

22 5

YHTE EACR A LOT TUBOA CAHE HETRO

.

57 39 6 51 49

HYET KTEA CARE OF CEAH OHETR

.

8 50

OUY EWHRT YWAA MY SAENJ

?

16 38 34 2 26 59 29 30 46 47 54 33

EW ELFE IGULTY UATBO ATHT

.

10 21

HTWA NI TEH LORDW RAE OYU NGNISGI

?

12

ELT'S DO AREESRCH NO MISDOI

' .

18 14 1 31 37 24 13 40 60 45 27 23 15 58 36 20 19 41 32 48 28

Secret Message:

1 2 3 4 5 6 7 8 9 10 11 12 13 14 15 16 17 18 19 20 21 22 23 24 25 26 27 28

29 30 31 32 33 34 35 36 37 38 39 40 41 42 43 44 45 46 47 48 49 50 51 52 53 54 55 56

57 58 59 1 8 9 0 .

60

10. Public Speaking

Sit on the Hot Seat

Answer questions from your classmates. See Appendix C on page 193 for sample questions.

Make a Speech

Prepare a five minute speech on one of the following topics. See Appendix D on page 194 for more information.

- The recycling program where I live
- What is Earth Day?
- The dangers of global warming
- Think globally, act locally – what we can do to help the environment
- Where does our garbage go?

Note: Search the Internet if you need to get extra information.

Keep an Inventory
Add to:
Expression Clusters—Appendix E
Expression Collections—Appendices F and G

Lesson 8

Time to Say Good-Bye

Theme: The Last Class

Warm-Up

1. This is the last class of an English program. What are some possible questions that everyone is asking?
2. The class in the cartoon is in an English-speaking country. How is this similar to your own class? How is it different?

Focused Listening

Before You Listen

In the cartoon, the teacher is going around the circle and asking students questions. What are some possible questions that she is asking?

As You Listen

Ⓐ Close your book. Listen to the conversation between the teacher and students to find the answers to these questions.

What are they talking about? Why?

Ⓑ Listen again, but this time listen while you read the conversation.

TEACHER: OK. We have a few more people to ask. Carmen, what are you doing **over the break**?

CARMEN: Well, my best friend will be here for two weeks and I'm going to **show her around**. I can't wait to see her.

TEACHER: Well, that sounds really nice. There's so much to do around here, I'm sure you'll have a great time. And Danny, how about you?

DANNY: I don't have anything planned.

TEACHER: Really?

DANNY: Well, I was going to go back home, but **it didn't work out**.

TEACHER: What happened?

DANNY: I didn't get my ticket early enough, and now the prices are really high.

TEACHER: That's happened to me before. To get a good price, you really need to get your ticket **far in advance**.

DANNY: I know. But I think I'**m better off** stay**ing** here anyway so I can work more on my English.

TEACHER: Wow! **That's music to my ears!** Good for you, Danny! And now, Mei, what are you going to do over the break?

MEI: Nothing much. I have to work. I have a part-time job.

TEACHER: Well, **at least** you won't have any homework for awhile!

HIROSHI: Do *you* have any plans for the break?

TEACHER: Uh huh, and I'm really looking forward to it. I'm going to take it easy, take walks, go to the movies, visit friends, read . . . Oh! Wow! Look at the time! It's time to go and I hate to say good-bye. I hope you all **got a lot out of** our class, and that you'**ll keep in touch**. Have a great break, and **above all**, don't forget to speak English!

After You Listen

(A) Read the sentences about the conversation. Circle *T* for *true*, *F* for *false*, or *?* if you don't know.

1.	The teacher starts with Carmen when she asks questions.	T	F	?
2.	Carmen isn't going away for the break.	T	F	?
3.	Danny got a cheap airplane ticket the last time he flew home.	T	F	?
4.	Danny will work on his English during the break.	T	F	?
5.	Mei is going to work during the break, but her teacher isn't.	T	F	?

(B) **Guess the Meanings**

Below is a list of paraphrases of five of the idiomatic expressions in the conversation. On your own or with a partner, try to guess the five. To do this, make sure that what is written below would easily fit in the conversation.

Paraphrase	Idiomatic Expression
1. very early	______________________
2. most importantly	______________________
3. be her tour guide	______________________
4. That's wonderful!	______________________
5. benefited from	______________________

(C) Say the conversation in groups of five. Then have one group of students say the conversation in front of the class.

Understanding the New Expressions

Work with Others

If you're working with a partner or in a small group, read the short dialogues and examples for each expression aloud. Also, complete the Your Turn exercises together. For each expression, circle *Yes* or *No* to show if you understand. If you circled *No*, highlight or underline what is unclear, and ask questions for clarification.

Figure It out on Your Own

Read the short dialogues and examples for each expression. Also, complete the Your Turn exercises that don't need partners. Then, for each expression, circle *Yes* or *No* to show if you understand. If you circled *No*, highlight or underline what is still unclear, and ask questions in class for clarification.

1. **over the bréak** = *during* the time between sessions of classes; for some students and teachers, this is a time for vacation.

A: What did you do **over the break**?
B: We worked for a week, and then we went away for a few days.

Similar Expressions: **over vacátion, over the wéekend, over the súmmer**

- What did you do **over (your) vacation**?
- I have a lot of work to do **over the weekend.**
- We went swimming a lot **over the summer.**

Note: Notice that when you use "over," the phrase refers to one time, not a routine:

Over **(one specific time)**	***On*** **(general or repeated times) (Use *in* with seasons.)**
• I plan to read a lot *over vacation*. (one vacation in the future) • What are you going to do *over the weekend*? (next weekend) • What did you do *over the summer*? (last summer)	**Notice present tense for routine.** • I always read a lot when I'm *on vacation*. (every vacation) • What do you usually do *on weekends*? (most weekends; notice the plural) • What do you usually do *in the summer*? (any summer)

Your Turn

Complete the chart with information about you and one of your classmates. Write complete sentences with the bolded expressions.

Questions	You	Your Classmate
What are you going to do **over the next break?**	I'm going to . . .	
What are you going to do **over the weekend?**	I'm going to . . .	
What do you usually do **on weekends?** (= every weekend)	I usually . . .	

2. **shów someone aróund (somewhere)** = take someone to see the different parts of an area

ALL CLEAR ? Yes No

- Let me know when you're in town. I'd love to **show you around**.
- Our friends didn't have time to **show us around**, so we took a bus tour.
- We were busy all weekend with out-of-town visitors. We **showed them around** all day Saturday and Sunday.

Similar Expression: **trável aróund** = travel from one place to another—here and there

A: What are you going to do this summer?
B: I'm going to work for a month, and then I'm going to **travel around** California with a friend for two weeks.
A: Where are you going to go?
B: We're not sure. Probably San Francisco, Yosemite, Los Angeles. We'll see.

Yosemite is a national park in California.

3. **It dídn't work óut.** = Something that was planned didn't happen.

ALL CLEAR ? Yes No

They were going to

- get married,
- buy a house,
- take a trip,
- visit us,

but **it didn't work out.**

Grammar Notes:

- You can use similar forms of this expression: I hope your plans **work out**; I think it **will work out**; Maybe it **won't work out**, but I'm going to try to do it.
- The past continuous tense *(was going to/were going to)* is often used to talk about a plan that didn't happen:
  He was *going to* go to the beach for the weekend, but **it didn't work out** because it rained.

Contrast: **work óut** = exercise

- She's going to the gym to **work out**. She **works out** three times a week.

Your Turn: Listening Challenge

Listen to find out what **worked out** and what **didn't work out**. Then, complete the chart.

A *camp counselor* is usually a teenager who works at a camp and takes care of children.

Situation	Did it work out?	Why or why not?
1. summer camp last year		
2. getting married		
3. car/truck		

4. **(fár) in advánce** = **(fár) ahéad of tíme** = early; before the scheduled time
   - The teacher told them about their test **far in advance (far ahead of time)** so they would have a lot of time to study.
   - Can they pay you **in advance (ahead of time)**?
   - Can you let me know **in advance** what time you'll be here? I want to be sure to be home.
   - The meeting is on Tuesday. How **far in advance** do you want me to give you the information?

5. **be bétter off** = be in a better situation (than another situation) ≠ **be wórse off**

   Grammar Note: This expression is used to show a comparison, and it is often followed by gerunds, prepositions, and time words.

Gerunds	• We'**re better off being** early than late. • You'**re better off taking** three classes than four.
Prepositions	• He'**s better off with** that car (than without it). • She'**s better off without** that expensive apartment. • We **aren't better off in** this apartment than in that one. • They **were better off in** 1998 (than they are now).
Time Words	• Think about two years ago. **Are** you **better off** or **worse off now**? • We **were better off two years ago**.

Your Turn

Interview five members of your class. Ask each student: *Are you better or worse off now than you were three years ago? Why?* Take short notes in the column on the right. After you finish your interviews, write five sentences about your classmates. Follow the example below.

Student first name	Better off	Worse off	1 to 3 reasons
Example: Dan	✓		married now + better job

Example sentence: Dan is better off now than he was three years ago because he's married and he has a better job.

1. ______________________________

2. ______________________________

3. ______________________________

4. ______________________________

5. ______________________________

6. **Thát's músic to my éars!** = That's wonderful! That's great news! (You say this in response to something that you *hear.*)

A: We'll miss you two.
B: I didn't tell you? We decided not to move.
A: Really? I can't believe it! **That's music to my ears!**

7. **at léast** = Use this expression to show that there is a good side in a situation with a problem.

Problematic situation	***at least . . .* (good point)**
1. I have to work over the break.	But **at least** you won't have homework.
2. It rained, so we had to move the party from the yard to the house.	**At least** you still had the party.
3. He doesn't like his job.	Well, **at least** he *has* a job!

Contrast: **at least** = the minimum number; not less than

TEACHER: Your essay is due next Monday.
STUDENT: How many pages should it be?
TEACHER: **At least** five.

A: How many people do you think came to the show?
B: Oh, I think **at least** 500.

Your Turn

Work with a partner and come up with your own problematic situations. Then point out the bright side—something good. Follow the examples in the box above.

Problematic situation	***At least . . .* (good point)**
1. ______________________	**At least** ______________________
2. ______________________	**At least** ______________________
3. ______________________	Well, **at least** ______________________

8. **gét a lót out of something** = learn a lot about something or get pleasure from doing something ≠ **gét nóthing out of something**

A: How did you like the book?
B: It was great. I **got a lot out of** it.

A: How did you like the books?
B: They were great. I **got a lot out of** them.

- It was a great { experience / book / class / lecture / trip } and I **got a lot out of** it.
- The lecture was OK, but I **didn't get a lot out of** it.
- I **got nothing out of** the movie because I couldn't understand anything. They were speaking so fast!

Your Turn

Talk to a partner about a class that you got a lot out of in the past. Then, talk about an experience that you got nothing out of. Give reasons.

9. **kéep in tóuch (with) = stáy in tóuch (with)** = stay in contact with ≠ **lóse tóuch (with) (past = lost)**

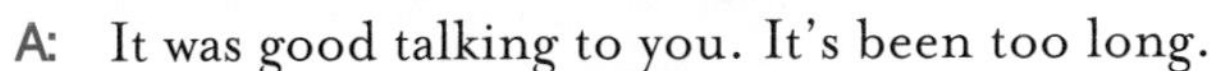

A: It was good talking to you. It's been too long.
B: I know. We really need to **keep (stay) in touch**.

A: Do you know how they're doing?
B: I have no idea. We **lost touch with** each other a few years ago.

> lose ≠ find;
> loose ≠ tight
>
> The 's' in *lose* sounds like 'z.' The 's' in *loose* sounds like 's.'

Similar expressions: **be in tóuch (with)** ≠ **be óut of tóuch (with); be/gét báck in tóuch (with)** = **be/gét in tóuch** again

A: **Are** you **in touch with** him?
B: No, we**'ve been out of touch** for two years.

A: I thought you two **lost touch.**
B: We did, but we **got back in touch** when we saw each other at the party.

Your Turn

Who are you in touch with? Who aren't you in touch with? Complete the sentences with names of friends and people in your family. Then, talk to a partner. Give details about why and how you are in touch and why you aren't in touch.

1. I keep in touch with ______________________________.
2. I don't want to lose touch with ______________________________.
3. I don't stay in touch with ______________________________.
4. I lost touch with ______________________________.
5. I'm out of touch with ______________________________.
6. I was out of touch with ______________________________, but now we're back in touch.
7. I want to get in touch with ______________________________.

You can be in touch *by e-mail, by phone,* etc.

10. above áll = most importantly; more important than anything else

- I love all kinds of food, but **above all**, I love my mom's cooking.
- My parents taught me to be a good person and **above all**, to always tell the truth.
- (Teacher) You're going to learn a lot of vocabulary and grammar in this class. But **above all**, you're going to gain confidence in your ability to speak English.

NEW EXPRESSION COLLECTION

over the break	in advance	get a lot/nothing out of
over vacation	ahead of time	keep/stay/be/get back in touch
on vacation	be better/worse off	be out of touch
show around	That's music to my ears!	lose touch
travel around	at least	above all
work out		

Exercises

(See page 179 for pronunciation exercises for Lesson 8. Focus: Voiced and Voiceless Consonants and the -s Ending.)

1. Mini-Dialogues

Read the sentences in Column A. Choose the *best* response from Column B. Not all responses can be used.

When checking this exercise in class, perform each mini-dialogue. One student should read an item from Column A, and another student should read the response from Column B.

1A	1B
___ 1. Don't wait until the night before the test. Study in advance!	a. Showing my cousins around. They're visiting for a week.
___ 2. Where have you been all day?	b. Great. I got a lot out of it. You should read it.
___ 3. The party's at 8:00. Remember to bring the cake. And above all, get here ahead of time!	c. I think she's working out at the gym.
___ 4. How was the book?	d. That's good advice. I hope I can follow it!
___ 5. Our day worked out very well. First we went to a museum, and then we had dinner. We spoke English the whole time.	e. That's music to my ears!
___ 6. Where is she?	f. Don't worry. I'll be there before 7:00.
	g. We're still in touch.

2A	2B
___ 1. He was going to live alone, but then he decided he'd be better off sharing the rent with a roommate.	a. I hope it works out. He's hard to live with!
___ 2. I'm so tired. Over the weekend, we painted the whole house.	b. It didn't work out for right now. We're going to go over the summer.
___ 3. Have you heard from her?	c. I know. She would be a lot worse off if she were unemployed.
___ 4. What are you doing here? I thought you went back to your country.	d. Well, at least it's done. How does it look?
___ 5. She complains a lot about her job, but at least she has a job.	e. Get in touch when you're back, OK?
	f. No. I sent her three e-mails and she didn't answer. Maybe she doesn't want to stay in touch.

2. Grammar Practice

Follow the directions and complete the sentences.

Directions	Sentences
1. Add a preposition.	a. What do you usually do ______________ weekends?
	b. What did you do ______________ the weekend?
	c. Can you get here ahead ______________ time?
	d. I hope they get back ______________ touch when they get back from their trip.
	e. We've been out ______________ touch for ages. I think I'll e-mail him.
	f. It was a great experience and I got a lot out ______________ it.
	g. Let me know when you're coming. I need to know ______________ advance.
	h. That's music ______________ my ears!
	i. She didn't win, but ______________ least she tried.
	j. He's better off ______________ Ann than Jan.
	k. He's better off ______________ Jan because they argue a lot.
	l. They were worse off ______________ 1999.
	m. I'd love to see your house. Can you show me ______________?
2. Add a past tense verb.	a. I just got an e-mail from her. She finally ______________ in touch!
	b. I haven't heard from him in years. We ______________ touch a long time ago.
	c. They ______________ in touch for a long time, but then they stopped e-mailing each other.
	d. Do you think people ______________ better or worse off ten years ago?
	e. They ______________ us around their house and we were very impressed. I got some new ideas for my house.
	f. We were going to go dancing last night, but it (negative) ______________ out.

3. Error Correction

Find the errors and make corrections.

1. What are you going to do on the break?
2. People better off a long time ago.
3. He got a lot out his music class.

4. We wanted to go, but it didn't worked out.
5. I plan to show around the city my friends.
6. They were out touch for a long time, but they're back in touch now.
7. Be sure to be here ahead time.
8. I'm so glad to hear that. That music to my ears!
9. What do you usually do over the weekends?
10. She working out three times a week.

4. Choosing the Idiom

Today is the last day of Hiroshi's music class, and he is talking to Emily, one of his classmates. On page 150, fill in the blanks with the best possible expressions from the list. Pay special attention to how the expressions are used grammatically. You may need to consider verb tenses, subject-verb agreement, pronouns, prepositions, etc. Not all of the expressions can be used. After you finish, practice reading the dialogue aloud.

keep in touch with	above all	get a lot out of
lose touch	work out	get nothing out of
at least	(not) work out	over the break
show _ around	in advance	be better off

EMILY: It's hard to believe that classes are over. What are you going to do (1) ______________________?

HIROSHI: Sleep.

EMILY: Me, too. We're all so tired!

HIROSHI: That's the truth. Are you going to go anywhere?

EMILY: Uh-huh. I'm going to visit my parents. They just retired and moved, and they want to (2) ______________________.

HIROSHI: That sounds good.

EMILY: How about you?

HIROSHI: I was going to travel around for a few weeks with my friend, but unfortunately it (3) ______________________. He can't go, so I'm just going to stay here.

EMILY: And sleep.

HIROSHI: Right. (4) ______________________ I'll have the time to sleep. And I plan to go to the gym and (5) ______________________ ______________________ a lot. I've been lazy and now it's time to get serious about exercise.

EMILY: Well, with all that sleep you're going to get, you'll have a lot of energy. Do you have any plans to go back to Japan?

HIROSHI: Uh-huh, in six months. I decided that I (6) ______________________ ______________________ staying here the whole time so I can work on my English.

EMILY: Do you ever get homesick?

HIROSHI: Uh-huh. But I (7) ______________________ everyone a lot by e-mail, and I found a cheap phone card. And my best friend was here last month.

EMILY: Well, that's good. Are you planning to take music again next semester?

HIROSHI: Yes, for sure. I (8) ______________________ this class, and I really want to continue. I've learned a lot about music, and (9) ______________________, it's been good for my English. How about you?

EMILY: Oh, music is my major, so I'll definitely be here. Well, it was great talking to you, Hiroshi. I hope you have a great break! See you in a few weeks!

HIROSHI: OK. Have a great time!

5. Sentence Writing

This time, in this exercise, you will not write *about* the paragraphs. Instead, you will just rewrite the paragraphs with expressions from the box. (**Bolded** words and phrases in the story represent where expressions can go.) Underline the expressions that you use.

Remember to pay attention to grammar details: verb tenses, prepositions, articles, singular and plural nouns, etc.

Hi, everyone! Congratulations on finishing, or almost finishing, this book! I hope you **learned a lot from it**. And if you're going to have a test soon, I hope you **won't wait until the last minute to study**!

When you finish your English course, maybe you're going to have a break. I hope that **during your break**, you'll get some rest. If you're not going to travel or do anything special, **it's good that** you'll have some free time.

I also hope that you're planning to **stay in contact with** some of your classmates. Maybe you'll e-mail and call each other. And maybe some of you will **visit each other and see new places**. If you do, I hope you'll communicate in English and use some of the expressions you learned. If I ever hear you use any of these expressions, I'll say **"That's wonderful to hear!"**

Good luck as you continue to learn English. Keep paying attention to idioms and other expressions. They make a language more interesting. And **more than anything else**, as you study English, have confidence in yourself and have a good time!

That's music to my ears!	keep in touch with	in advance
over your break	show ____ around	above all
get a lot out of	at least	

Start with: *Hi, everyone! Congratulations on finishing, or almost finishing, this book! I hope you . . .*

6. Dictation

You will hear the dictation three times. First, just listen. Second, as you listen, write the dictation on a piece of paper. Skip lines. Third, look at Appendix A on page 184 to check what you have written.

7. Questions for Discussion and/or Writing

(For more detailed instructions, see Lesson 1, Exercise 7.)

Discussion: You can answer these questions orally in groups or in the *Walk and Talk* activity in Appendix B on page 192.

Writing: You can write your own answers to these questions, or you can write the responses that you received from students during the *Walk and Talk* activity.

Questions

1. Describe your dream vacation. Use your imagination and give details. Where will you be? Why? Who will you be with? Why? What will you do? Why?
2. Some people say that a vacation is for relaxation, but that traveling takes energy and can be hard work. If you had three weeks off, how would you spend it—relaxing, traveling, or both? Explain.
3. Do you work? If yes, do you get any time off for vacation? How much?
4. When you have free time, what do you usually do? If you will have a break soon, what will you do?
5. When you make plans, do you usually make them in advance or are you more spontaneous and wait until the last minute? Explain.
6. Think of someone from about ten years ago that you have lost touch with. Would you like to get back in touch? Why or why not?

Culture Note

Working Americans often get just two weeks of vacation a year. What is the typical amount of vacation time in your native country? Do you think it is enough?

Sentence Starters:

1. *My dream vacation is to be in* _____ (OR: *is to go to* _____).
2. *I would spend a three-week vacation* _____*ing . . .*
3. *I get* _____ *weeks off a year.*
4. *When I have free time, I . . .*

   If I have a break soon, I will . . .
5. *I usually make plans . . .*
6. *I lost touch with* __ *and would (not) like to get back in touch because . . .*

8. Walk and Talk

In the cartoon, students are walking around their classroom, asking each other about their plans for a break, and sometimes about their plans for their future.

Do the same in your class. Greet and talk to at least five different students. Ask about their plans. In your conversations, try to use some expressions from this lesson. Refer to or write on the board the New Expression Collection on page 146. Also, try to use other expressions that you know. But don't feel that it is necessary to have an idiom in every sentence.

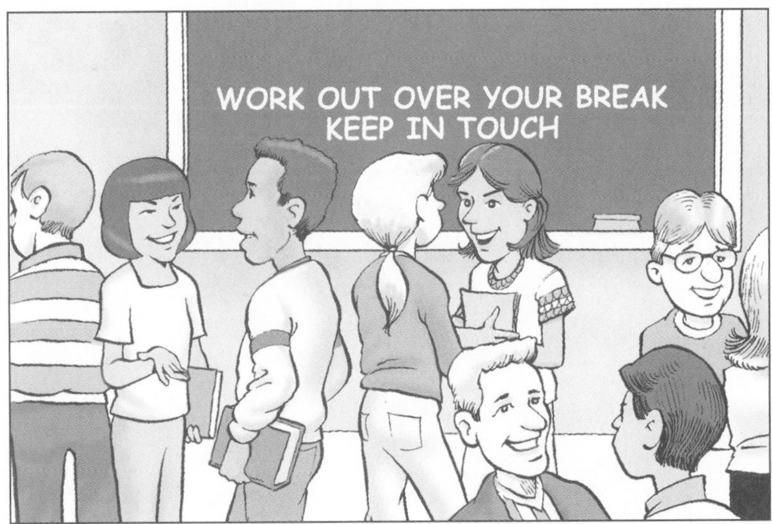

Possible starting line: *Carmen, what are you going to do over the break?*

9. Tic-Tac-Toe

See detailed directions on page 113.

get a lot out of	**lose touch**	**be better off**
. . . At least . . .	**in advance**	**. . . Above all, . . .**
work out	**show _ around**	**over the weekend**

10. Public Speaking

Sit on the Hot Seat

Answer questions from your classmates. See Appendix C on page 193 for sample questions.

Make a Speech

Prepare a five minute speech on one of the following topics. See Appendix D on page 194 for more information.

- My dream vacation
- A vacation I once took
- How to get a lot out of being a student
- How to get a lot out of being in a different country

Note: Search the Internet if you need to get extra information.

Keep an Inventory
Add to:
Expression Clusters—Appendix E
Expression Collections—Appendices F and G

Review — Lessons 7 and 8

Collocation Match-Up

Collocations are special combinations of words that can be idioms or other phrases and expressions. Find collocations from *Lessons 7* and *8* by matching the words from Column A with words in Column B. (You will probably be able to make additional expressions that are not from Lessons 7 and 8. Put these in the box.)

A		B
1. feel guilty	________________	show you around
2. be guilty	________________	of that course
3. pay your bills in	________________	doing a good job
4. run out	________________	to my ears
5. get a lot out	________________	your notes
6. what in the world	________________	ahead of time
7. let me	________________	advance
8. care about	________________	out of the cookie jar
9. do research on	________________	of that garbage
10. I hope it'll work	________________	about forgetting
11. that's music	________________	care of yourself
12. go through	________________	in touch
13. get here	________________	out for you
14. take your hand	________________	of a serious crime
15. be better	________________	least it's not raining
16. get rid	________________	butterflies
17. take	________________	up after the party
18. let's keep	________________	of sugar
19. at	________________	off changing our plans
20. clean	________________	is going on

Additional Collocations

Review — Lessons 7 and 8

Crossword Puzzle

Across

2 Promise to get ___ in touch when you're back in town!

5 I didn't like the book. I got nothing ___ of it.

6 Don't worry. I took care ___ it.

7 She ___ guilty about not cleaning up after the party.

9 He told her that ___ all, she has to stop missing class.

11 They're doing ___ on idioms for their class project.

12 She just ___ out that she got the job.

Down

1 It's bad now, but we'll be ___ off if we don't get any rain soon.

3 If you visit, let me know in ___ so I can make plans.

4 When we were going ___ some old pictures, we found a picture of you!

6 I hope I'll see you ___ the summer.

8 Sorry! I ___ your paycheck away by mistake!

10 When are you coming to visit? I want to show you ___.

12 We got to the airport ___ ahead of time, so we went to a restaurant.

How are you doing? Complete the Self-Evaluation Questionnaire in Appendix H on page 203. Use the Study Tips in Appendix I on page 204.

Pronunciation

LESSON 1: Getting Cold Feet

Sentence Stress

This exercise will help you learn which words are usually, but not always, stressed (emphasized) in a phrase or sentence. Stressed words are the most important words in phrases and sentences because they carry the most information. Native speakers of English stress words that are the most important by making them stronger than the other words. They do this by making the stressed syllables in these words longer.

Look at some lines from the introductory conversation. The stressed words are capitalized and the unstressed words are not capitalized.

ELLEN: Can you BELIEVE it JANA? Your WEDDING is in TWO WEEKS!

JANA: I KNOW.

ELLEN: WHAT'S WRONG?

JANA: WELL . . . I THINK I'm GETTING COLD FEET.

ELLEN: Oh, DON'T WORRY. THAT'S NORMAL. THAT'S HOW I FELT BEFORE I MARRIED TIM. But EVERYTHING will be FINE. You and RICK are REALLY GREAT TOGETHER.

JANA: I KNOW, but MAYBE we should WAIT. We CAN'T EVEN AFFORD to BUY FURNITURE!

> Pronouns are usually not stressed. "I" is not stressed even though it is always capitalized.

Now, look at the charts with words from this conversation. Notice that whether a word is stressed or not relates to its "part of speech."

Parts of Speech That Are *Usually* Stressed

Nouns	Main verbs	Negative helping verbs	Adjectives	Adverbs	*Wh*-words	This/That These/Those
Jana wedding weeks feet Tim everything Rick furniture	believe know think getting worry felt married wait afford	don't can't	two wrong cold normal fine great	well before really together maybe even	what how	that

Parts of Speech That Are *Usually* Unstressed

Pronouns	Possessive adjectives	Forms of *be**	Affirmative helping verbs	Conjunctions	Prepositions	Articles	Infinitive "to"
you it I we	your	is am are	can am will should	but and	in	a an the	to buy

*The verb *be* is stressed when it is the last word in a sentence. (Yes, I WAS.)

Practice 1

With a partner, practice saying the first part of the introductory conversation on page 157. Make the capitalized words (except "I") stronger than the other words.

Practice 2

Read the rest of the introductory conversations below. Underline the words that you think should be stressed. If you are not sure about the part of speech of a word, ask yourself if the word is important to communicate the meaning of the sentence. Words like "to" and "in" don't have as much *content* or meaning as words like "marry" and "change."

ELLEN: Oh, so, it's money that's making you have second thoughts. But deep down you really want to get married.

JANA: You're right. I really do. I'm dying to marry Rick.

Words like *Oh* and *Uh-oh* are stressed.

TIM: Hey, Rick. What's wrong?

RICK: I don't know. I just hope I'm ready to get married.

TIM: Uh-oh! Are you getting cold feet?

RICK: I guess you could say that. I'm about to change my life for good, so I'm kind of nervous.

TIM: OK. Then call off the wedding.

RICK: But I'm dying to marry Jana!

TIM: And she's dying to marry you. So why don't you just take a deep breath and calm down!?!

Practice 3: Listen and Speak

1. Go through the *Understanding the New Expressions* section of Lesson 1 and analyze where stress marks are used in each expression. Say each expression aloud.
2. Listen to the introductory conversations on page 2 and focus on which words are stressed.
3. Listen again, sentence by sentence, and repeat what you hear.
4. Listen to the recorded mini-dialogues in Exercise 1 on page 11. Focus on which words are stressed. Repeat what you hear. Then, say each mini-dialogue with a partner.

LESSON 2: Pulling an All-Nighter

Part 1: Stress in Phrasal Verbs

Phrasal verbs are composed of verbs + words such as *in, on, at, up, down, out,* and *about.* Many of these small words are prepositions.

In this exercise, you will learn to stress (emphasize) the second part of phrasal verbs. You learned in Lesson 1 that we don't usually stress prepositions and other small words. In phrasal verbs, however, we make an exception—we stress these words.

Grammar Points to Remember About Phrasal Verbs

- Some phrasal verbs, such as *stay up,* cannot be separated. They are called "inseparable." That means that you cannot put words between *stay* and *up.*
- Some phrasal verbs can be separated. They are called "separable." You can put words between them. For example:

He handed in his homework.	She handed back the tests.
He handed *his homework* in.	She handed *the* tests back.
He handed *it* in.	She handed *them* back.

- When you use a pronoun with a separable phrasal verb, the pronoun has to be in the middle of the phrasal verb. It cannot come after it. And remember that pronouns are not usually stressed.

Incorrect: ~~He handed in it.~~ ~~She handed back them.~~

Practice 1

Say these phrasal verbs from Lessons 1 and 2 aloud. Make the capitalized words stronger and louder than the other words. Don't stress the pronouns.

call OFF	call it OFF
calm DOWN	calm her DOWN
hand IN	hand it IN
turn IN	turn them IN
hand BACK	hand them BACK
hand OUT	hand it OUT
stay UP	

Practice 2

Listen to the sentences about a student named Joe. Repeat what you hear. Then, with a partner, practice saying the sentences.

1. Sometimes Joe *stays* UP all night before a test.
2. He gets very nervous when his teachers *hand* OUT tests.
3. He gets very nervous when his teachers *hand them* OUT.
4. He's even more nervous when his teachers *hand* BACK his tests because he's worried about his grades.
5. He's even more nervous when they *hand them* BACK.
6. He doesn't always *hand* IN his homework because he doesn't always do it.
7. His teacher sometimes collects homework, but he doesn't always *hand it* IN.
8. He promises that next year, he'll *turn* IN all of his work.
9. When he gets homework next year, he'll *turn it* IN.
10. Once Joe got an 'A,' and he got so excited that he couldn't *calm* DOWN.
11. He studied for the test because his soccer game was *called* OFF.
12. His coach *called it* OFF because of rain.

Part 2: Stress in Compound Nouns

Compound nouns, sometimes called *noun compounds,* are nouns with two words. The two words can be

- together *(handout)*,
- separate *(high school)*, or
- separated by a hyphen *(T-shirt)*.

Whether compound nouns are composed of words that are together or separate, the stress pattern is the same. Stress the first word in compound nouns. Stress in phrasal verbs is the opposite—you stress the second word.

Compound noun: HANDout Phrasal Verb: hand OUT

Practice 1

Say these compound nouns aloud. Stress the capitalized words or parts of words.

School-related compounds	**Other compound nouns**
HANDout	NEWSpaper
HOMEwork	WEBsite
NOTEbook	LOVE story
COLLEGE student	TEENager
CLASSmate	POSTcard
CLASSroom	POST office
ENGLISH teacher	PAYcheck
BLACKboard	PAYday
CHALKboard	T-shirt
WORKsheet	BABY-sitter

Practice 2

Listen to the sentences about Joe's brother, Jack. Repeat what you hear. Stress the capitalized words and parts of words. Then, with a partner, practice saying the sentences.

1. Jack is a COLLEGE student and he's very different from his brother, Joe.
2. Jack always does his HOMEwork on time, and his ENGLISH teacher thinks he's a great student.
3. Unlike Joe, Jack is very organized. You should see his NOTEbook. He has all of his HANDouts organized by date.
4. When his teacher writes on the BLACKboard, Jack takes notes.
5. He helps his CLASSmates when they need help.

Part 3: Stress in Phrasal Verbs and Compound Nouns

Listen to the story about two brothers, Jack and Joe. Repeat what you hear. Stress the capitalized words and parts of words. Then, with a partner, practice saying the sentences aloud.

Jack is a COLLEGE student, but he's still a TEENager. He works hard and is very organized. When his teachers hand OUT WORKsheets and other material, Jack always puts them in his NOTEbook according to the date. That way, when he needs to look at a particular HANDout, he can find it easily.

Jack's brother, Joe, is different. He's still in HIGH school, and he doesn't work very hard in school. But he works hard at his job. He delivers NEWSpapers early in the morning, and he's always happy on PAYday when he gets his PAYcheck. In the evenings, he often stays UP late and looks at different WEB sites.

Jack was similar to Joe when he was in HIGH school. Maybe Joe will change when he becomes a COLLEGE student.

LESSON 3: Are We Couch Potatoes?

Part 1: Reduced Forms

As you know, many words that you have difficulty understanding in fast speech are easy to recognize when they are written in their full forms. One reason for your difficulty in understanding is that native speakers often "reduce" the full forms when they speak.

It is not necessary for you to learn how to pronounce reduced forms. What is more important is for you to recognize and understand them when you hear them.

Practice 1

Listen and repeat this list of the full and reduced forms that appear in the introductory conversation in Lesson 3 (pages 40–41) and in Exercise 4 (pages 50–51). (When a reduced form has more than one syllable, the stressed syllable is in capital letters.)

2,21

Full form	Pronunciation of reduced form
let me	LEM-me
going to	GON-na / GO-ing ta / GO-in ta/
want to	WAN-na / WAN-ta
to	ta
of	a
a couple of	a-COU-ple-a
and	'n
safe and sound	SAFE-'n-SOUND
you	ya
what do you	WA-da-ya

Practice 2

Listen and repeat. Pay special attention to how the underlined words are pronounced.

1. Here, let me take your coats.
2. What movies are we going to see tonight?
3. Want to guess what they are?
4. You don't want to become a couch potato, do you?
5. Lucy wants to get together with me three times a week and take walks.
6. Get home safe and sound.
7. We all need to relax.
8. We'll surprise you with a couple of great classics.
9. What do you feel like doing?

Practice 3

2,23 Listen and say the "pair words" listed below. Pay special attention to the shortened pronunciation of the word *and*.

Nouns
bread 'n butter
men 'n women
peace 'n quiet
pros 'n cons

Verbs
wait 'n see
forgive 'n forget

Adjectives
safe 'n sound
short 'n sweet
bright 'n early

Part 2: Contractions

Contractions are two words that are put together to form one word. Native English speakers use many contractions when they speak, and that may be one reason why you sometimes don't understand what you hear.

Practice 1

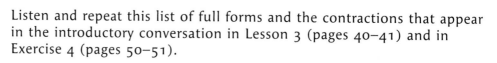

2,24 Listen and repeat this list of full forms and the contractions that appear in the introductory conversation in Lesson 3 (pages 40–41) and in Exercise 4 (pages 50–51).

Full forms	Contractions	Vowels sound like
It is	It's	'i' as in *sit*
You are	You're	'o' as in *or*
I am	I'm	'y' as in *my*
Do not	Don't	'o' as in *no*
Does not	Doesn't	'u' as in *up*
We are	We're	*ear*
We will	We'll	'ee' as in *see*
There is	There's	*air*
Let us	Let's	'e' as in *yes*
Where is	Where's	*air*

Practice 2

Listen and repeat. Pay special attention to how the underlined contractions are pronounced.

1. It's so good to see you!
2. Oh, you're so thoughtful!
3. I'm so glad we can finally get together.
4. It's been such a long time.
5. I'm in the mood for something funny.
6. I don't feel like watching anything serious.
7. It's healthy to laugh.
8. Do you think we're couch potatoes?
9. It doesn't matter what we watch.
10. Listen, there's no need to worry about being a couch potato.
11. Let's watch a movie.
12. It's getting late.
13. We'll surprise you with a couple of great classics.
14. I don't want to spend all my time reading.
15. Where's the remote?

Part 3: Reduced Forms and Contractions

Practice: Listen and Speak

1. Underline the reduced forms and contractions in the introductory conversation in Lesson 3 (pages 40–41) and in Exercise 4 (pages 50–51).
2. Listen to the two conversations and focus on the reduced forms and contractions.
3. Listen again, sentence by sentence, and repeat what you hear.

Intonation in Statements and Questions

You stress words that carry the most information, usually nouns, main verbs, adjectives, and adverbs. But one of these words will carry the most meaning in each phrase, clause, or sentence. That word, in addition to being stressed, should also be given the highest intonation (pitch) in a sentence. That word often contains *new* information for the listener.

Intonation, the rising and falling of your voice, helps you communicate meaning. High intonation communicates new information or what you think is most important, very high intonation communicates emotional feelings, and low intonation indicates that a sentence is ending. If you don't vary your intonation in English, you may give the impression that you are bored, and the people listening to you won't necessarily catch your meaning.

Intonation is the rising (going up) and falling (going down) of a speaker's voice.

Part 1: Intonation in Statements

Intonation usually goes

1. up on the stressed syllable of the most important word, and down at the end of a sentence to show that the sentence is ending.

   It was a HARD day.

2. up and then down at the end of a sentence if the last word in the sentence is the most important one. The stressed syllable on this word receives the highest intonation.

   It might not come back on till to MOR row.

If the last word in a sentence has only one syllable, that word is said longer.

I'll go out of my M I N D.

Practice

Practice using rising-falling intonation with sentences from the Lesson 4 introductory conversation. Listen and repeat.

1. I'm so glad you CAL L ED.

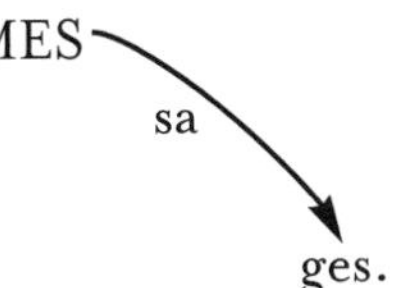

2. Sorry honey, I just checked my MES sa ges.

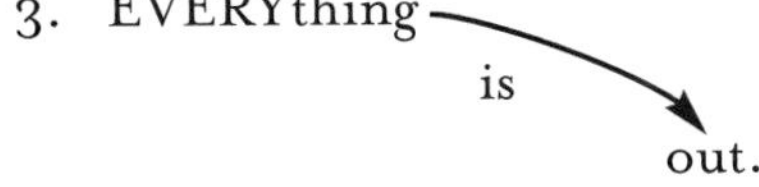

3. EVERYthing is out.

4. I'm sorry that I'm not THERE with you and MAG gie.

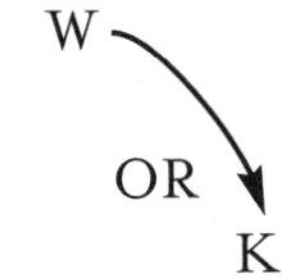

5. I think I have about one more hour to W OR K.

Part 2: Intonation in Questions

Intonation usually goes

1. up and then down at the end of *wh-* (information) questions.

   Where were you?

2. up at the end of *yes-no* questions.

   Are the lights still out?

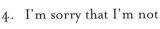

Practice 1: Intonation in *Wh*-Questions

Listen and repeat. Practice using rising-falling intonation with *Wh*-questions from the introductory conversation in Lesson 4 (page 56).

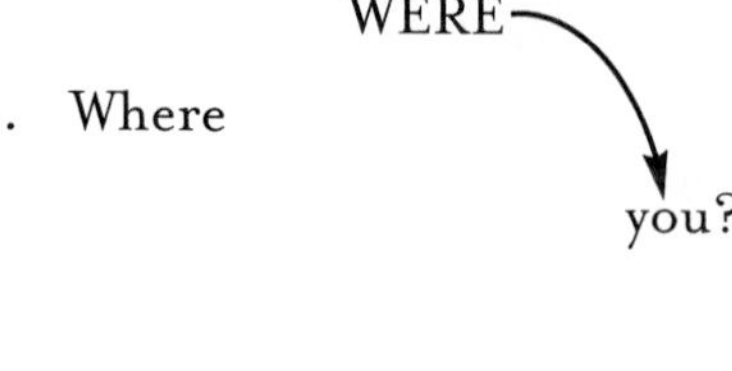

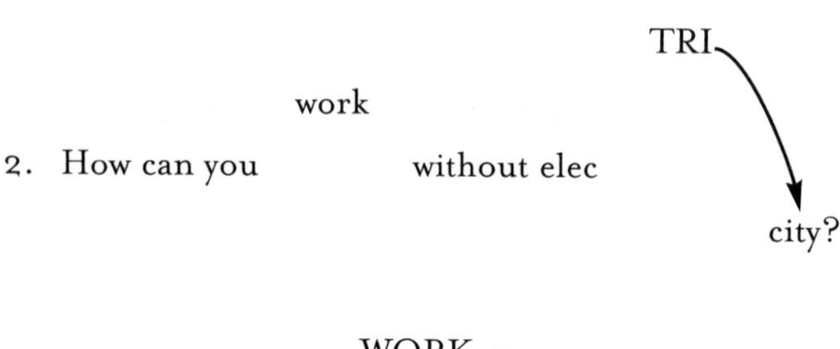

TRI
work
2. How can you
without elec
city?

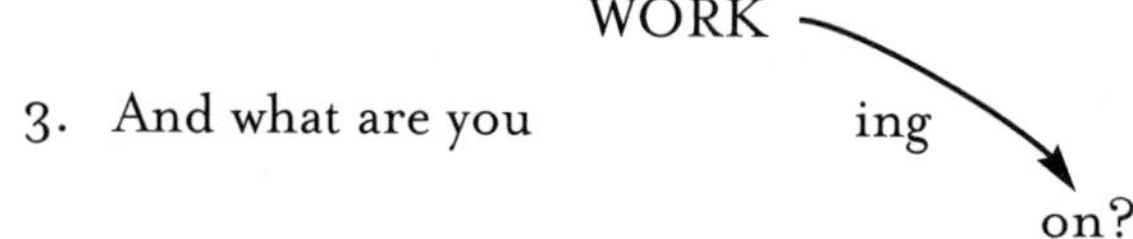

Practice 2: Intonation in *Yes-No* Questions

2,29

Listen and repeat. Practice using rising intonation with *Yes-No* questions from the introductory conversation in Lesson 4 (page 56).

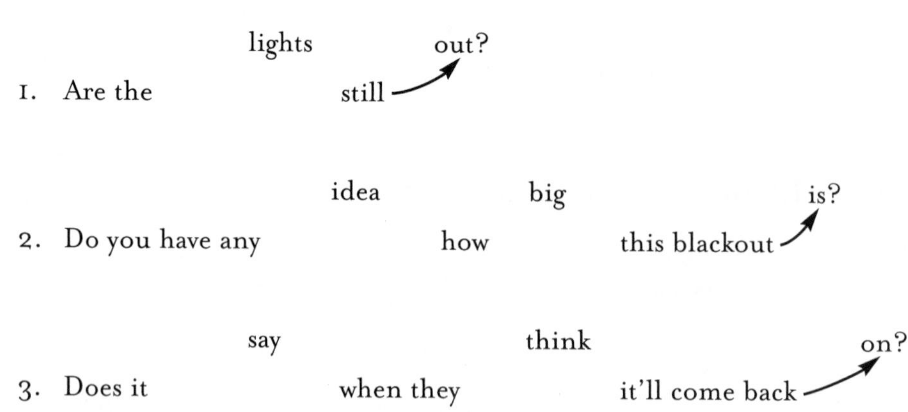

lights
out?
1. Are the
still
idea
big
is?
2. Do you have any
how
this blackout
say
think
on?
3. Does it
when they
it'll come back

Part 3: Intonation in Statements and Questions

Practice: Listen and Speak

1. Read the introductory conversation in Lesson 4 on page 56. Put down arrows (↓) at the end of every statement and *Wh-* question. Put up arrows (↑) next to each *Yes-No* question.
2. Listen to the conversation and focus on the rising and falling intonation used by the two speakers.
3. Listen again, phrase by phrase or sentence by sentence, and repeat what you hear.

2,30

LESSON 5: Workaholic Mom

Stress and Intonation Review

Practice 1

1. Review the rules about sentence stress (Lesson 1, pages 157–158) and intonation (Lesson 4, pages 166 and 167).
2. Below is the beginning of the conversation in Exercise 4 from Lesson 5. As you say the conversation with a partner, do the following:

2,31

- Stress the capitalized words and syllables—make them longer, stronger, and louder than other words.
- Make your voice go up and down. The up/down arrows remind you to use rising-falling intonation with statements and *Wh*-questions. The up arrows remind you to use rising intonation with *Yes-No* questions.
- "Law firm" and "cooking school" are compound nouns (see pages 160–161). As you know, you need to stress the first word in a compound noun. You also need to give the first word higher intonation:

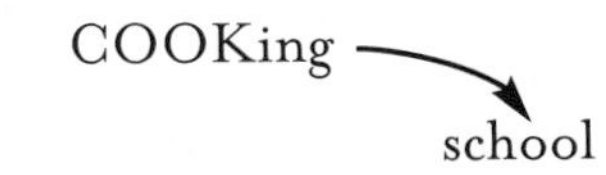

(↑↓) (↑↓) (↑)

PAT: WELL MOM, I TOLD you I HAVE a surPRISE. Are you REAdy?

(↑↓)

ROSEMARY: I've been WAITing ALL NIGHT.

(↑↓) (↑↓) (↑↓)

PAT: OK. WELL, HERE it IS. I'm QUITting my JOB at the LAW firm, and

(↑↓)

I'm GOing to CHANGE caREERS!

(↑↓) (↑↓) (↑↓)

ROSEMARY: WHAT? My GOODness, WHAT do you HAVE in MIND?

(↑↓)

PAT: You KNOW I'm DROWNing in WORK I DON'T LIKE. And you KNOW I've

(↑↓)

NEVer BEEN REALly HAPpy as a LAWyer. So I've deCIded to GO to

(↑↓)

COOKing school.

(↑) (↑↓)

ROSEMARY: COOKing SCHOOL? But you alREADY HAVE a GREAT JOB! HOW can I TALK

(↑↓)

you OUT of DOing THIS?

2,32

Practice 2: Listen and Speak

1. Read this adaptation of Exercise 5 from Lesson 5.
2. Listen to the recording, and focus on the speaker's stress and intonation.
3. Listen again, phrase by phrase or sentence by sentence, and repeat what you hear.
4. With a partner, take turns reading the paragraphs.

Hi everyone! I'm Jerry and I'd like to talk to you about a problem I had. I used to be a workaholic, but don't worry—I'm OK now.

I had my own business, and I did well. In fact, I was swamped with work. Whenever anyone asked me to go to the movies or out to dinner, I always asked for a rain check.

I always stayed in my office late because I kept saying, well, I'll get one more thing over with. And I never took a day off. It didn't make a difference if I was sick. I still went to work. And I have to be honest, every day when I woke up, I really looked forward to going to the office.

Then one day, my family told me that I needed help. I asked them what they had in mind—a psychiatrist? And they told me that I needed to talk to somebody—not necessarily a psychiatrist—because I didn't have a healthy life. Wow! Was I surprised to hear this! I thought about what they said, and kept going back and forth about getting some help. Then my son talked me into making an appointment.

Well, I was lucky to get really good advice. Now I'm through with being a workaholic. I still work, but I spend more time with my family and friends. After all, they are the most important people in my life.

LESSON 6: Guess Who?

Part 1: Thought Groups and Rhythm

Look at A and B below from the introductory conversation in Lesson 6. Which shows the best way to say the lines?

__ A or __ B

A

PETER: (Guess) (who)?

LAURA: (Oh)! (I) (can't) (believe) (it)! (I) (know) (it's) (you), (Peter!) (I) (haven't) (seen) (you) (in) (ages). (How) (are) (you)?

B

PETER: (Guess who)?

LAURA: (Oh)! (I can't believe it!) (I know it's you,) (Peter!) (I haven't seen you) (in ages.) (How are you?)

The answer is that *B* is better. Each group of words in parentheses in *B* expresses a thought and is called a *thought group.* By saying each group of words without pausing between the words, we create a certain rhythm.

At the end of each thought group, our voices go down in pitch and we sometimes pause briefly.

If you say each word equally with pauses between them, you won't be using English rhythm. This can make your English difficult to understand, even if you are using clear pronunciation of sounds and correct grammar and vocabulary.

Question: How can you know which words make up a thought group?

Answer: What goes into a thought group can vary, so it's not possible to give rules for 100 percent of the time. But you can follow these general guidelines:

Words often in a thought group	**Example**
• a short sentence or question	*I know it's you.* *Guess Who?*
• a phrase (a group of words)	*for a few minutes*
• words that go alone (exclamations, transitions)	*Oh!* *However, . . .*

In writing, commas, periods, and other punctuation marks indicate the ends of thought groups. These markers help make written language more understandable. In speech, changes in pitch and short pauses make our spoken language more understandable to our listeners.

Practice 1

Say the beginning lines of Lesson 6 introductory conversation line by line, in thought groups.

Guess who?

Oh!
I can't believe it!
I know it's you,
Peter!
I haven't seen you
in ages
How are you?

Pretty good.
How about you?

Fine.
Busy as always.
You know me.
I'm such a workaholic.
Wow!
It's really great to see you.
I'd love to catch up
on your news

Do you have time
to sit down?
Or were you
on your way out?

I was leaving,
but I can join you
for a few minutes.

Great!
So tell me,
how's your family?

Practice 2

Look at the rest of the introductory conversation in Lesson 6 on page 96. With a partner, rewrite the dialogue line by line in thought groups, in the same form as it is written in Practice 1. Don't be afraid to guess. It is possible to arrange thought groups differently. Say the words in the thought groups to yourself to see if they feel naturally grouped. Then, say the entire conversation with your partner.

Part 2: Linking

Linking means connecting. In English, we often link words within thought groups. That may be one reason why you may not always understand what you hear, but are able to understand the same words when they are written.

The following are some of the situations in which we link words:

1. when a word ends in a consonant *sound* and the next word starts with a vowel *sound*. ("Believe" ends in the *letter* 'e,' but the final *sound* is the consonant 'v.')

   Believe‿it or not, . . . It turned‿out that . . .

   /v/ /ɪ/ /d/ /aʊ/

2. when a word ends in a vowel *sound* and the next word starts with a consonant *sound*.

Sounds vs. Spelling

Be careful not to confuse letters from the alphabet and actual sounds. When you are linking words, look at and listen for the sounds rather than the letters.

Look at the word *university*. It starts with the vowel letter *u*, but the first sound in this word is really */y/*. Also look at the word *hour*. It starts with the consonant letter *h*, but the first sound in this word is really the vowel */au/*. And don't let words that end in silent vowels fool you. The last letter in the word *come* is *e*, but the last sound is really */m/*.

Practice 1

Add linking lines to the thought groups in Practices 1 and 2 in Part 1 on pages 172–173. Practice saying the thought groups aloud again, but this time also focus on linking.

For example:

I can't believe‿it!

I know‿it's you,

Practice 2: Listen and Speak

1. Listen to the recording of the introductory conversation in Lesson 6 on page 96. Focus on thought groups and linking.
2. Listen again, phrase by phrase or sentence by sentence, and repeat what you hear.
3. With a partner, take turns reading the conversation.

Practice 3: Listen and Speak

1. Read this adaptation of Exercise 5 from Lesson 6.
2. Listen to the recording and focus on the speaker's use of thought groups and linking.
3. Listen again, phrase by phrase or sentence by sentence, and repeat what you hear.
4. With a partner, take turns reading the paragraphs.

Hi! You know me—I'm Sue. I know we haven't talked in ages and you said that you want to catch up on my news. Well, believe it or not, I'm not a vegetarian anymore. I know, I know. You think I'm kidding, but I'm not. Maybe I'll change again down the road, who knows?

Well anyway, I'm sure you want to know the rest of my news. Listen to this—when I was at a restaurant with my friend Martin last week, I thought I saw our English teacher. I was scared, but I went over to her table to say hello. When I got there, it turned out that it wasn't my teacher. I was really embarrassed, as you can imagine.

There isn't much else to talk about. I keep busy with schoolwork and my part-time job. And I'm applying to college.

I know I've been talking to you for ages and you need to go. Thanks for listening!

LESSON 7: Don't Throw It Away—Recycle!

Voiced and Voiceless Consonants and the *-ed* Ending

The final *-ed* that is used to form the past tense of regular verbs can have three sounds: the voiceless /t/, the voiced /d/, or a new syllable /ɪd /. To determine which sound to use, you need to know whether the last sound (not letter) of a word is voiced or voiceless. All vowel sounds are voiced.

You can feel whether consonant sounds are voiced or voiceless by holding your hand against your throat and saying the sounds. If you feel a vibration, the sound is voiced.

Don't feel that it is necessary to memorize the chart below. It is for your reference. The best strategy for you when working on your pronunciation is to listen very carefully to the speech of native speakers.

See Appendix J, Guide to Pronunciation Symbols, on page 205.

CONSONANTS

Letters	Sounds	Voiced	Voiceless	Example
b	/b/	x		**b**ut
c	/k/		x	**c**omputer
	/s/		x	scien**c**e
d	/d/	x		**d**inosaur
f	/f/		x	**f**orget
g	/g/	x		for**g**et
	/ʤ/	x		technolo**g**y
h	/h/		x	**h**ome
j	/ʤ/	x		**j**udge
k	/k/		x	thin**k**
l	/l/	x		mai**l**
m	/m/	x		progra**m**
n	/n/	x		wo**n**
p	/p/		x	com**p**uter
q	/kw/		x	**q**uite
r	/r/	x		**r**eally
s	/s/		x	u**s**
	/z/	x		i**s**
	/ʒ/	x		u**s**ual
t	/t/		x	grea**t**
v	/v/	x		**v**ery
w	/w/	x		**w**on
x	/ks/		x	si**x**
y	/y/	x		**y**ou
z	/z/	x		**z**oo
ch	/tʃ/		x	**ch**ange
	/ʃ/		x	ma**ch**ine
	/k/		x	te**ch**nology
sh	/ʃ/		x	**sh**e
th	/ð/	x		**th**is
	/θ/		x	**th**ink
ng	/ŋ/	x		thi**ng**

-*ed* Past Tense Ending Rules

Final sound of regular verb	Pronunciation of -*ed* ending	New syllable added?	Examples
voiceless	/t/	no	*asked* = /æsk**t**/
voiced	/d/	no	*cleaned* = /klin**d**/
/t/ or /d/	/ɪd/	yes	*started* = /stártɪ**d**/
			decided = /dɪsáɪdɪ**d**/

Practice 1*

Look at the list of some of the regular verbs from the Lesson 7 introductory conversation, Exercise 4 dialogue, and dictation.

- Say the base form of each verb. Write the final *sound* of each of these verbs on the lines.
- If the final sound is /t/ or /d/, then circle the /Id/ past tense ending in the column on the right.
- For all the other base forms of verbs, decide if the final sound is voiced or voiceless. (Remember that all vowel sounds are voiced. For consonant sounds, look at the chart on page 176.)
- Circle whether the past tense forms of these verbs should end in the voiceless /t/ or voiced /d/ sound.
- With a partner, say both the base form and past tense form of each verb.

Base form of regular verb	Final sound	Past tense	Final *-ed* sound
1. believe	v	believed	/t/ (/d/) /ɪd/
2. notice	____	noticed	/t/ /d/ /ɪd/
3. try	____	tried	/t/ /d/ /ɪd/
4. help	____	helped	/t/ /d/ /ɪd/
5. care	____	cared	/t/ /d/ /ɪd/
6. want	____	wanted	/t/ /d/ /ɪd/
7. start	____	started	/t/ /d/ /ɪd/
8. happen	____	happened	/t/ /d/ /ɪd/
9. need	____	needed	/t/ /d/ /ɪd/
10. ask	____	asked	/t/ /d/ /ɪd/

**The answers to Practice 1 appear on page 221 in the Pronunciation Answer Key.*

Practice 2*

2,35

- Read the following paragraphs silently. As you read, write above the underlined words how to pronounce the *-ed* endings: /t/, /d/, or /ɪd/.
- Look at the words that follow the *-ed* sounds. If any of these words start with a vowel sound, write linking lines between the *-ed* and the vowel sound that follows. (See page 173 for information on linking.)
- After you have finished marking these paragraphs, listen to how they sound on the audio program.
- Take turns reading the paragraphs aloud with a partner.

Michael, Kathy, and Lee were cleaning up after a meeting when

/t/

Michael suddenly noticed that Kathy was throwing a glass bottle away. He started yelling because she wasn't recycling and he asked her if she cared about the environment. He talked about what he learned when he did some research on the lack of places for garbage, and this made Kathy feel guilty.

Lee suggested that they all go through the garbage bags and take out the bottles. She offered to take them home and recycle them. But they decided that all three of them would take bottles home. They agreed that this was the best thing to do.

Practice 3: Listen and Speak

1,5; 1,10; 1,15; 1,20; 1,25; 2,5; 2,10; 2,15

The dictations in Appendix A are mostly in the past tense. Choose a dictation from a lesson that you have already studied, and underline regular past tense verbs. Then, near each of these verbs, mark which of the three *-ed* endings you think you should use: /t/, /d/, or /ɪd/.

Listen to the dictation to check, and then practice saying the past tense verbs aloud. When you are ready, dictate the paragraph or paragraphs to a partner or small group.

**The answers to Practice 2 appear on page 221 in the Pronunciation Answer Key.*

Voiced and Voiceless Consonants and the *-s* Ending

The final *-s* is used to indicate:

- the third person singular form of verbs (visit**s**)
- possessives (Carmen's)
- regular noun plurals (week**s**)

These *-s* endings can have three sounds: the voiceless /s/, the voiced /z/, or a new syllable, /ɪz/.

To determine which sound to use, you need to know whether the last sound (not letter) of a word is voiced or voiceless. All vowels are voiced.

To find out whether particular consonant sounds are voiced or voiceless, look at the consonant chart on page 176.

-s Ending Rules

Sound of word	Pronunciation of -s ending	New syllable added?	Examples	
voiceless	/s/	no	*waits* =	/weɪts/
voiced	/z/	no	*happens* =	/hǽpɪnz/
s, z, sh, ch, j, x	/ɪz/	yes	*classes* =	/klǽsɪz/
			relaxes =	/rilǽksɪz/

Practice 1*

Look at some of the regular nouns from the Lesson 8 introductory conversation and Exercise 4 dialogue.

- Say the singular form of each noun. Write the final sound of each noun on the lines.
- If the final sound is *s, z, sh, ch, j,* or *x,* then circle the /ɪz/ final sound in the column on the right.
- For all the other singular nouns, decide if the final sound is voiced or voiceless. (Remember that all vowels are voiced. For consonant sounds, look at the chart on page 176.)
- Circle whether the plural forms of these nouns should end in the voiceless /s/ or voiced /z/ sound.
- With a partner, say both the singular and plural form of each noun.

Singular noun	Final sound	Plural noun	Final -*s* sound		
1. week	k	weeks	(/s/)	/z/	/ɪz/
2. friend	____	friends	/s/	/z/	/ɪz/
3. ticket	____	tickets	/s/	/z/	/ɪz/
4. price	____	prices	/s/	/z/	/ɪz/
5. break	____	breaks	/s/	/z/	/ɪz/
6. job	____	jobs	/s/	/z/	/ɪz/
7. plan	____	plans	/s/	/z/	/ɪz/
8. movie	____	movies	/s/	/z/	/ɪz/
9. parent	____	parents	/s/	/z/	/ɪz/
10. exercise	____	exercises	/s/	/z/	/ɪz/
11. gym	____	gyms	/s/	/z/	/ɪz/
12. card	____	cards	/s/	/z/	/ɪz/

**The answers to Practice 1 appear on page 222 in the Pronunciation Answer Key.*

Practice 2*

Look at some of the verbs from Lesson 8 introductory conversation and dictation.

- Say the base form of each verb. Write the final sound of each verb on the lines.
- If the final sound is *s, z, sh, ch, j,* or *x,* then circle the /ɪz/ final sound in the column on the right.
- For all the other base forms of verbs, decide if the final sound is voiced or voiceless. (Remember that all vowels are voiced. For consonant sounds, look at the chart on page 176.)
- Circle whether the third person singular forms of these verbs should end in the voiceless /s/ or voiced /z/ sound.
- With a partner, say both the base form and third person singular form of each verb.

Base form of verb	Final sound	Third person singular form	Final -*s* sound		
1. ask	k	asks	(/s/)	/z/	/ɪz/
2. show	____	shows	/s/	/z/	/ɪz/
3. wait	____	waits	/s/	/z/	/ɪz/
4. sound	____	sounds	/s/	/z/	/ɪz/
5. work	____	works	/s/	/z/	/ɪz/
6. happen	____	happens	/s/	/z/	/ɪz/
7. get	____	gets	/s/	/z/	/ɪz/
8. stay	____	stays	/s/	/z/	/ɪz/
9. look	____	looks	/s/	/z/	/ɪz/
10. take	____	takes	/s/	/z/	/ɪz/
11. visit	____	visits	/s/	/z/	/ɪz/
12. keep	____	keeps	/s/	/z/	/ɪz/
13. practice	____	practices	/s/	/z/	/ɪz/
14. relax	____	relaxes	/s/	/z/	/ɪz/
15. hope	____	hopes	/s/	/z/	/ɪz/

**The answers to Practice 2 appear on page 222 in the Pronunciation Answer Key.*

Practice 3*

- Read the following paragraphs silently. As you read, write above the underlined words how to pronounce the *-s* endings—as */s/*, */z/*, or */ɪz/*.
- Look at the words that follow the *-s* sounds. If any of these words start with a vowel sound, write linking lines between the *-s* and the vowel sound that follows. (See page 173 for information on linking.)
- After you have finished marking these paragraphs, listen to how they sound on the audio program.
- Take turns reading the paragraphs aloud with a partner.

2,36

/ɪz/

When English classes‿end, it is common for students and their teachers to talk about their plans during their breaks. Some students take trips and others stay home. Sometimes students have visitors and they show them around. And some students work because their vacations from their jobs are different from their school vacations.

My friend's brother never takes vacations. The only time he relaxes is when he watches TV. He works almost all the time. When he has free time, he washes his car and fixes things around his house. And I know he exercises every day at the gym.

As for me, well, I always find time to relax!

**The answers to Practice 3 appear on page 222 in the Pronunciation Answer Key.*

Appendices

Appendix A: Dictations (Exercise 6)

Exercises 3 and 5 from the Answer Key can be used as additional dictations.

Your teacher will put the key words on the board to help you with spelling.

Lesson 1, Page 15

Two weeks before they got married, Jana and Rick were in a swimming pool talking to their best friends. At one end of the pool, Jana was telling her friend Ellen that she was getting cold feet because they couldn't even afford to buy furniture. Ellen told Jana that she shouldn't have second thoughts about marrying Rick because deep down she really loved him.

At the other end of the pool, Rick was telling his friend Tim that he was nervous because he was about to change his life for good. Then when Tim told Rick to call off the wedding, Rick said he was dying to marry Jana.

Clearly, both Rick and Jana were nervous about getting married and they needed to calm down.

Lesson 2, Page 33

Annette is having a bad day. She's very tired because last night she pulled an all-nighter writing a paper. Luckily she finished it in the nick of time, so it wasn't late. But she didn't do well on a surprise quiz in her history class because her mind went blank. Her friend Alan told her to go home and take a nap, but Annette said she had to study for another test. Alan didn't say this, but he thinks Annette needs to hit the books more.

Lesson 3, Page 51

Two couples got together to watch some movies. After they made themselves comfortable, they started talking. They said they felt like watching the comedy first because they needed to laugh after a hard week at work. Then Susan told everyone that her sister called her and Michael *couch potatoes.* It's true that they spend a lot of time watching TV.

After they watched two movies, the hosts thanked Susan and her husband for coming. It was a rainy night, but Susan and Michael got home safe and sound.

Lesson 4, Page 69

Dave is away on a business trip, and Carla is at home with their daughter Maggie. It's evening, and there's a big blackout. Carla is working on a report almost in the dark. She's working by candlelight and Maggie is sound asleep.

When Dave called, he got online to give Carla information about the blackout. He said that it looked like the power was out in more than five states.

Carla told him that she couldn't wait for the blackout to be over. She said she would go out of her mind if it lasted a long time.

Lesson 5, Page 90

Rosemary is the new director of a very big company. When her daughter Pat invited her to dinner for her birthday, she asked for a rain check because she was swamped with work. But Pat talked her into meeting her for dinner on Thursday. Rosemary said that she would get her work over with before then so she could go out.

Pat wasn't sure about where to go for dinner. She had two places in mind, and she was going back and forth between them. She wanted the dinner to be special for two reasons. First, because it was her mother's birthday. And second, because she was going to surprise her mother with some news when they were through with dinner.

Both Rosemary and Pat were looking forward to having dinner together.

Lesson 6, Page 111

On his way out of a restaurant, Peter ran into his old friend Laura. They hadn't seen each other in ages, so they caught up on each other's news. Peter's four children keep him and his wife very busy, and Laura's work keeps her busy. Peter couldn't believe it when Laura told him that her husband works at home. Peter liked this idea and said that maybe he would do the same thing down the road. After Peter left, Laura spent the rest of her lunch hour reading the newspaper.

Lesson 7, Page 133

Michael, Kathy, and Lee were cleaning up after a meeting when Michael suddenly noticed that Kathy was throwing a glass bottle away. He got angry because she wasn't recycling, and he asked her if she cared about the environment. He said that he had done research and found out that we're running out of places to put our garbage. He made Kathy feel very guilty.

Lee suggested that they all go through the garbage bags and take out the bottles. She said that she would take them home and recycle them. But they decided that all three of them would take bottles home and recycle them there.

Lesson 8, Page 151

During their last English class, students and their teacher talked about what they were planning to do over the break. One student is going to show her best friend around, and another student is going to work because she has a part-time job.

Another student, Dan, isn't going back to his country because he didn't get a ticket far enough in advance. Now the tickets are too expensive. At least while he's here, he can practice his English.

Their teacher plans to relax during the break, and she told her students that she hopes that they got a lot out of the class. She also hopes that everyone will stay in touch and remember to speak English while they're on vacation.

Appendix B: Walk and Talk Forms (Exercise 7)

Directions

- Put the names of the students you talk to in the spaces on the left.
- Ask each person no more than two questions. Then move on to someone else.
- Don't ask the same question more than once.
- Write very short notes in the spaces after each question. Don't write full sentences. Write just enough so you remember what your partners said. As you write, try to frequently look up at the person you are talking to.
- After you have completed this activity, write what your classmates said on a separate sheet of paper. As you write, be sure to include the new expressions in your sentences when possible. To check what you have written, you can *Walk and Talk* again and show your writing to the students you interviewed.

Lesson 1, Page 15

__________________ 1. Did you ever get cold feet before a big event? If yes, what happened—did you change your plans, or did you deal with the scary situation?

__________________ 2. Some American people have superstitions about getting married. Do you have superstitions related to wedding customs in your native country? What are they?

__________________ 3. Deep down, do you *really* want to learn English, or are you studying it because (a) your school requires it, (b) your parents want you to learn it, or (c) it is necessary for your work?

__________________ 4. What is something that you are dying to do within the next five years? Why?

Lesson 2, Page 34

________________ 1. Have you ever pulled an all-nighter? If no, why not? If "yes, where? When? What class was it for? What did you do to stay awake?

________________ 2. What kind of study habits do you (or did you) have as a student? That is, do you hit the books every night or do you cram at the last minute?

________________ 3. (a) What is the best way to study for a test on idioms and expressions? (b) Have you ever taken a test cold? If yes, explain the situation. (c) Has your mind ever gone blank during a test? If yes, explain what happened. (d) In your native country, do teachers often give surprise pop quizzes? What is your opinion of surprise quizzes?

________________ 4. In your native country, can students turn in their work late? If they can turn their work in late, what is the penalty? That is, do they get a lower grade?

________________ 5. Describe a situation in which you were (or someone you know was) in hot water. What happened?

Lesson 3, Page 52

__________________ 1. Do you know any couch potatoes? If yes, who? Are you one? How much TV do you watch every day? What kind of show is your favorite?

__________________ 2. Do you think parents should limit how much TV their children watch? How many hours a day are OK? Should parents limit how many hours a day children spend playing video games or using the Internet?

__________________ 3. How can parents prevent their children from watching TV shows that contain sex and violence?

__________________ 4. When you watch TV in English, do you turn on the closed-captioning so that you can read what the people are saying? If yes, how does this help you?

__________________ 5. When you see a movie that was made in a foreign language, do you prefer subtitles (words in your native language written at the bottom of the screen) or dubbing (words in your native language that are spoken)? Explain.

__________________ 6. Who do you think holds the remote control more—men or women? Why?

__________________ 7. Do you think it's possible to be addicted to the Internet? Do you know any *mouse potatoes*?

Lesson 4, Page 70

________________ 1. Do you use the Internet? If yes, how often do you get online? How often do you check your e-mail? What kinds of Web sites do you like to visit? Do you go to sites that are in your native language or in English, or both?

________________ 2. Do you have any projects that you're working on now? If yes, what are they? What are you planning to work on in the future?

________________ 3. What are you going to do when this program or semester or school year is over? How do you think you'll feel?

________________ 4. What kinds of things bother you? In other words, what makes you go out of your mind?

________________ 5. Are you from an area where there are natural disasters such as hurricanes, tornadoes, floods, or earthquakes? If yes, describe an experience you or someone you know had with an event.

________________ 6. What do you think people should do to prepare for an emergency situation? Have you already done this preparation or are you planning to?

Lesson 5, Page 90

________________ 1. How would you describe yourself when it comes to work? Rate yourself on a scale of 1 to 5.

1———————2———————3———————4———————5

lazy a little lazy moderate hardworking workaholic

________________ 2. Explain your answer to number 1: (a) Why did you give yourself this rating? (b) Does the amount you work relate to the type of work that you are doing? In other words, how hard do you work on your English? How hard do you work as a student in general? If you have a job, how hard do you work at your job?

________________ 3. In the introductory dialogue, Rosemary is talking on the phone and working on her computer at the same time. This is called "multitasking"—doing more than one thing at a time. Are you so busy that you "multitask?" If yes, give examples of things you do at the same time.

________________ 4. "All work and no play makes Jack a dull boy" is a proverb in English. The message is that hard work without time for fun and relaxation is not healthy. What are some proverbs or expressions related to "work" in your native language?

________________ 5. Many people in the United States get just two weeks of vacation a year. Some people see this as a reflection of the strong "work ethic" in American culture. How much is work valued in your native country? What is the average number of weeks of vacation that people get per year?

________________ 6. What do you think are the effects of "workaholism?" What are some ways to help people with this problem?

________________ 7. Imagine that you really want to go away for the weekend with your friend. But your friend doesn't want to go. Are you the kind of person who would try to talk your friend into going, or would you just forget the idea the first time your friend says no? If you would try to talk your friend into going, what would you say?

________________ 8. Have you ever tried to talk someone out of getting married, getting divorced, quitting a job, taking a job, quitting school, gambling, going somewhere, etc.? What happened?

Lesson 6, Page 111

________________ 1. Imagine that you are at a party. You are talking to someone you haven't seen in ages. What kinds of questions do you ask? What topics do you talk about?

________________ 2. Imagine that you are at a party. You are talking to someone you don't know, so you need to "make small talk." You talk about the party and the food, and maybe the weather. What else can you talk about? And how can you show that you are listening to the other person?

________________ 3. In the introductory dialogue, Peter says that his wife is home (and not at work) because she recently had a baby. Perhaps she is "on maternity leave." In your native country, is it common for women to "get maternity leave" from their jobs? If yes, for how long? Do men get "paternity leave?"

________________ 4. In the introductory dialogue, Laura says that her husband works at home and takes care of the shopping and cleaning. Some people might call him a "househusband." What do you think of this idea? Why?

________________ 5. What is something that you haven't done in ages that you would like to do again?

________________ 6. What is something that you have been doing for ages that you would like to stop doing?

________________ 7. What are your plans for after class? In other words, what do you plan to do for the rest of the day or evening?

Lesson 7, Page 133

_______________ 1. What do you do to help take care of the earth? Do you: recycle, avoid throwing garbage out of car windows, avoid littering? What other things can you and other people do?

_______________ 2. Are there recycling programs in your native country? If yes, what kinds of things are recycled? Explain how the recycling system works.

_______________ 3. Think of special things that you own and will never get rid of. These are things with "sentimental value." What are these things, and why do you want to keep them forever?

_______________ 4. What do you usually do to get rid of things you don't use anymore? Do you donate them to an organization? Do you give them to friends? Do you throw them away? Explain.

_______________ 5. If you had to do a research project, what would your topic be? Why?

_______________ 6. When you are invited to dinner at someone's house, do you offer to help clean up? Why or why not?

_______________ 7. What is one thing that you care a lot about? What is one thing that you don't care about at all?

_______________ 8. Imagine that some new students are coming to your English program. What do they need to find out about before classes start?

Lesson 8, Page 152

________________ 1. Describe your dream vacation. Use your imagination and give details. Where will you be? Why? Who will you be with? Why? What will you do? Why?

________________ 2. Some people say that a vacation is for relaxation, but that traveling takes energy and can be hard work. If you had three weeks off, how would you spend it—relaxing, traveling, or both? Explain.

________________ 3. Do you work? If yes, do you get any time off? How much?

________________ 4. When you have free time, what do you usually do? If you will have a break soon, what will you do?

________________ 5. When you make plans, do you usually make them in advance or are you more spontaneous and wait until the last minute? Explain.

________________ 6. Think of someone from about ten years ago that you have lost touch with. Would you like to get back in touch? Why or why not?

Appendix C: Hot Seat

Choose one student to come to the "Hot Seat" (a chair) in the front of the room. Or, get into groups and choose one student in each group to be on the "Hot Seat." This student will answer questions. Please avoid asking personal questions.

When you ask questions, remember to think about the rules for *Wh-* and *Yes-No* questions on page 167. (See Pronunciation section for Lesson 4.)

Possible questions

- What's your name?
- Where are you from?
- Why do you want to learn English?
- What are two things you do that help you learn English?
- What are your plans for the future?
- What do you do in your free time?
- Do you like to go to the movies? What kinds of movies do you like?
- Do you like to read? What kinds of books do you like to read?
- What is your favorite kind of music?
- What is your favorite kind of food?
- Describe a typical weekend. What do you usually do?

Appendix D: How to Make a Speech

Prepare a five minute speech about a topic that your teacher approves. Suggested topics appear at the end of each lesson. *Additional topics:* my job, a holiday in my native country, how to cook a special dish, etc.

Questions you might ask:

1. How will I know if my speech will be five minutes?

   The answer is: by practicing it *out loud* at home, even if you have to go into a room and close the door.

2. Can I read my speech?

   No. You will need to put short notes (not sentences) on note cards. (But you can write the first and last sentence on a card.) If you use more than one note card, number your cards.

3. How should I start and end my speech?

   To start, say "Today I'm going to talk about ___."

   To end, say "Thank you. Are there any questions?" (Don't end with "That's all.")

4. Can I memorize my speech?

   No. If you memorize your speech, it will sound like you are reading it. It is better to just look at notes and then make your own sentences.

5. How can I practice?

   - Find a quiet place.
   - Record your speech if you can.
   - Practice more than once.
   - Time your speech.

6. Can I change my topic?

   If you change your approved topic, you should talk to your teacher to make sure that your new topic is OK.

Sample note cards for speech

(You will probably need more than one card.)

①

Introductory Sentence: Today I'm going to talk about a typical wedding in my native country.

- show video clip and photos of my wedding
- how most couples meet
- what comes first—parties for a week
- preparations
  - bride's parents
  - groom's parents
  - the bride (who helps her, what she wears, etc.)
  - the groom (who helps him, what he wears, etc.)

②

- superstitions about weddings
- who's invited and the presents they bring
- the food
- entertainment

Conclusion: summary + my opinion of weddings in my native country.

(great time, see everyone, but not sure I want an arranged marriage)

Concluding Sentence: Thank you. Are there any questions?

(Please see the next three pages for speech evaluation forms—one for the teacher, one for a peer (a classmate), and one for you.)

SPEECH EVALUATION BY TEACHER

Name of Speaker: ______________________ **Grade:** ______________

	Disagree Strongly				Agree Strongly
1. The main idea was clearly stated.	1	2	3	4	5
2. Enough details were given to clarify the main idea.	1	2	3	4	5
3. The speech was well organized.	1	2	3	4	5
4. The speech was well prepared.	1	2	3	4	5
The speaker:					
5. showed interest in the topic.	1	2	3	4	5
6. glanced at brief notes and didn't read a written speech.	1	2	3	4	5
7. spoke clearly, at a moderate speed.	1	2	3	4	5
8. spoke in a voice that was neither too loud nor too soft.	1	2	3	4	5
9. recognized when it was necessary to define words and/or give an example.	1	2	3	4	5
10. used visual aids as necessary.	1	2	3	4	5
11. used eye contact effectively—that is, looked at people in all parts of the room.	1	2	3	4	5
12. used humor and smiled when appropriate.	1	2	3	4	5

Pronunciation Notes

____

____

Grammar/Vocabulary Notes

____

____

Comments

____

____

____

____

SPEECH EVALUATION BY CLASSMATE

Name of Speaker: ______________ **Name of Peer Evaluator:** ______________

NOTE: Each speech should have at least two peer evaluators.

	Disagree Strongly				Agree Strongly
1. The main idea was clearly stated.	1	2	3	4	5
2. Enough details were given to clarify the main idea.	1	2	3	4	5
3. The speech was well organized.	1	2	3	4	5
4. The speech was well prepared.	1	2	3	4	5
The speaker:					
5. showed interest in the topic.	1	2	3	4	5
6. glanced at brief notes and didn't read a written speech.	1	2	3	4	5
7. spoke clearly, at a moderate speed.	1	2	3	4	5
8. spoke in a voice that was neither too loud nor too soft.	1	2	3	4	5
9. recognized when it was necessary to define words and/or give an example.	1	2	3	4	5
10. used visual aids as necessary.	1	2	3	4	5
11. used eye contact effectively—that is, looked at people in all parts of the room.	1	2	3	4	5
12. used humor and smiled when appropriate.	1	2	3	4	5

I recommend that next time you ____

____

____

One thing very good about your speech was ______________________________

____

____

SPEECH SELF-EVALUATION

Name: ______________________________

	Disagree Strongly				Agree Strongly
1. The main idea was clearly stated.	1	2	3	4	5
2. I gave enough details to clarify the main idea.	1	2	3	4	5
3. My speech was well organized.	1	2	3	4	5
4. My speech was well prepared.	1	2	3	4	5
5. I showed interest in the topic.	1	2	3	4	5
6. I glanced at brief notes and didn't read a written speech.	1	2	3	4	5
7. I spoke clearly, at a moderate speed.	1	2	3	4	5
8. I spoke in a voice that was neither too loud nor too soft.	1	2	3	4	5
9. I recognized when it was necessary to define words and/or give an example.	1	2	3	4	5
10. I used visual aids as necessary.	1	2	3	4	5
11. I used eye contact effectively. That is, I looked at people in all parts of the room.	1	2	3	4	5
12. I used humor and smiled when appropriate.	1	2	3	4	5

If I could make this speech again, I would ______________________________

____

What I especially liked about my speech was ______________________________

____

Additional comments ______________________________

____

Appendix E: Expression Clusters

To help you remember expressions and the small words in them, add expressions to the "clusters" below. There are extra lines, so you can add other expressions that you talk about in class. Over time, you will see how many expressions with the same words you have learned. If you need more space, use index cards. Put one word on each card and add to the card as you move through *All Clear.*

Expressions with Verbs

MAKE — a difference

HAVE

TAKE — a nap

GET

BE

GO

DO

Expressions with Small Words

TO

AT

ON

OFF

UP

DOWN

OUT

IN

FOR

OF

BACK

OTHER

ABOUT

Appendix F: Expression Collection 1

Expressions from *All Clear 2* That Students Hear Or Read Outside of Class

Outside of class, you will hear and read many of the expressions that you are studying because the expressions are so common.

When you hear or read any of these expressions, write them down on an index card. This will help make you a more careful listener and reader, and you will find that you remember the expressions better.

It would be a good idea if perhaps once a week students in your class shared their lists.

EXPRESSION COLLECTION 1

Sentence with *All Clear 2* expression that I heard or read: ____________

____

____

Where I heard or read it: ______________________________

____

____

Who was speaking: ______________________________

____

____

Appendix G: Expression Collection 2

New Expressions That Students Hear Or Read Outside of Class

Outside of class, you will hear and read many expressions in English. You will find them on TV, on the radio, on the Internet, in the movies, on T-shirts, on bumper stickers, and in advertisements. They are everywhere.

Start a collection of these expressions by writing them down on index cards. You can find out what the expressions mean by asking someone outside of class or by asking your teacher.

It would be a good idea if perhaps once a week students in your class shared their lists.

EXPRESSION COLLECTION 2

Expression/Meaning/Sample Sentence: ______________________________

____

____

Where I heard or read it: ______________________________

____

____

Who was speaking: ______________________________

____

____

Appendix H: Student Self-Evaluation Questionnaire

Name (Optional): ______________________ **Date:** ____________

Circle the number that shows how much you agree or disagree with the sentences on the left.

	No		Yes
1. I know many more expressions in English.	1	2	3
2. Sometimes I try to use some of these expressions when I speak.	1	2	3
3. When I listen to native speakers of English, I sometimes hear expressions that I studied.	1	2	3
4. When I see or hear expressions that I don't know, I write them down and ask what they mean.	1	2	3
5. I know more about pronunciation in English.	1	2	3
6. I try to think about pronunciation when I talk.	1	2	3
7. I listen carefully to how native speakers of English pronounce words.	1	2	3
8. I'm working hard both in and outside of class.	1	2	3
9. I like to work with other students in class.	1	2	3
10. I like to study with other students outside of class.	1	2	3

Questions/Comments? ____

____

____

____

____

Appendix 1: Study Tips

1. Study Cards

Buy a set of 3″ x 5″ index cards. On each card, write the following with the expressions that you find most difficult to remember from each lesson.

Expression:

Sentence:

Grammar reminder:

Pronunciation reminder:

Example study card

Expression:	have second thoughts (about)
Sentence:	He had second thoughts about taking the job.
Grammar reminder:	Remember "about" + a noun or gerund.
Pronunciation reminder:	Tongue out a little for the "th."

2. Cover Your Walls

Do you ever wash dishes? Why don't you hang a card with expressions that you need to study near your sink? You can review while you wash dishes.

Of course, you can hang up cards all over your home. Soon you will be dreaming about expressions in English.

3. Other Ideas

(a) Write new expressions from in or out of class in a small book that fits in a pocket or purse. Study these expressions while you wait for a bus, wait to see a doctor, etc.

(b) Study with others. What are some of the ways you can study together?

____

____

____

(c) Your Suggestions?

____

____

____

Appendix J: Guide to Pronunciation Symbols

Vowels			Consonants		
Symbol	**Key word**	**Pronunciation**	**Symbol**	**Key word**	**Pronunciation**
/ɑ/	**hot**	/hɑt/	/b/	**boy**	/bɔɪ/
	far	/fɑr/	/d/	**day**	/deɪ/
/æ/	**cat**	/kæt/	/ʤ/	**just**	/ʤʌst/
/aɪ/	**fine**	/faɪn/	/f/	**face**	/feɪs/
/aʊ/	**house**	/haʊs/	/g/	**get**	/gɛt/
/ɛ/	**bed**	/bɛd/	/h/	**hat**	/hæt/
/eɪ/	**name**	/neɪm/	/k/	**car**	/kɑr/
/i/	**need**	/nid/	/l/	**light**	/laɪt/
/ɪ/	**sit**	/sɪt/	/m/	**my**	/maɪ/
/oʊ/	**go**	/goʊ/	/n/	**nine**	/naɪn/
/ʊ/	**book**	/bʊk/	/ŋ/	**sing**	/sɪŋ/
/u/	**boot**	/but/	/p/	**pen**	/pɛn/
/ɔ/	**dog**	/dɔg/	/r/	**right**	/raɪt/
	four	/fɔr/	/s/	**see**	/si/
/ɔɪ/	**toy**	/tɔɪ/	/t/	**tea**	/ti/
/ʌ/	**cup**	/kʌp/	/tʃ/	**cheap**	/tʃip/
/ɛr/	**bird**	/bɛrd/	/v/	**vote**	/voʊt/
/ə/	**about**	/ə'baʊt/	/w/	**west**	/wɛst/
	after	/'æftər/	/y/	**yes**	/yɛs/
			/z/	**zoo**	/zu/
			/ð/	**they**	/ðeɪ/
			/θ/	**think**	/θɪŋk/
			/ʃ/	**shoe**	/ʃu/
			/ʒ/	**vision**	/'vɪʒən/

Source: The Newbury House Dictionary of American English

Lesson Answer Key

Lesson Answer Key includes:

- As You Listen
- After You Listen
- Your Turn: Listening Challenge answers and scripts
- Exercises 1, 2, 3, 4, 5, 9

Lesson 1

As You Listen

- Jana is worried, especially about having enough money. But she really wants to marry Rick.
- Rick is also very nervous.

After You Listen

(A) T, F, ?, F, ?

(B) **Guess the Meanings**

1. can't afford to
2. be dying to
3. calm down
4. deep brown
5. for good

Your Turn: Listening Challenge

The woman is dying to be in an election. (She wants to "run for office.")

Script

PART A

A: Are you going to do it?

B: I'm not sure, but I'm really dying to.

A: Then what's the problem?

B: Well, it's expensive and I don't know if I can find enough money.

A: But you can try. A lot of people care about the same things you care about.

B: I know. But I need people around me that I can trust. Can you help me?

PART B

A: Sure. And I have some friends who can also help out.

B: OK. That's great. Then why don't we meet at my house on Sunday afternoon to plan?

A: Sounds good. I'll make some calls. Think positive! We're going to help you win this election!

Exercises

1. Mini-dialogues

1A/B: d, a, f, e, b
2A/B: b, f, c, a, d

2. Grammar practice

1.a. couldn't
1.b. had
1.c. got/had
1.d. were
1.e. were

2.a. going
2.b. taking
2.c. living
2.d. taking/accepting

3.a. to buy
3.b. to go/to live there, etc.
3.c. to see that movie/to have a vacation, etc.
3.d. to leave/to have dinner, etc.

4.a. of
4.b. of
4.c. about
4.d. for
4.e. about
4.f. off

3. Error correction

1. We didn't drive to New York because we <u>got</u> cold feet.
2. We had cold feet about <u>driving</u> there.
3. He <u>couldn't</u> afford an expensive present, so he bought her flowers.
4. Can you afford <u>to</u> live in San Francisco?
5. It's raining. I'm having second thoughts about <u>going</u> out tonight.

6. I'm dying to have an ice cream cone.
7. English is kind of hard.
8. We can't go to the party. They called it off ~~it~~.
9. He read the kids a story to calm them down.
10. I'm dying of thirst. Do you know where I can buy a bottle of water?

4. Choosing the idiom

1. cold feet
2. don't have second thoughts/ am not having second thoughts
3. am dying to
4. was about to
5. Calm down
6. kind of

5. Sentence writing (Answers can vary.)

1. Nancy **is dying to** leave her job because it's getting **sort of** boring.
2. Now she**'s having second thoughts about** changing jobs.
3. Sometimes she thinks she should stay at her old job **for good**.
4. She **can't afford to** buy a new car, but she needs one.
5. She needs to **calm down**.
6. Yesterday, when she **was just about ready to go out**, the phone rang.

9. Unscramble and find the secret message

HE IDDN'T TGE CDOL EEFT EBEORF SIH GWDDNIE.
HE DIDN'T GET COLD FEET BEFORE HIS WEDDING.

YTHE'RE NAISGYT ERTHE RFO GODO.
THEY'RE STAYING THERE FOR GOOD.

CLMA NDWO! I'LL LALC FOF EHT GWDIDEN.
CALM DOWN! I'LL CALL OFF THE WEDDING!

DEPE WDON, TYHE ODN'T TNAW TO OG.
DEEP DOWN, THEY DON'T WANT TO GO.

I SAW SUTJ TBUOA YDEAR OT AYS "YES," BTU I DDIN'T.
I WAS JUST ABOUT READY TO SAY "YES," BUT I DIDN'T.

NAER'T YOU IYNDG TO KETA A BAKRE?
AREN'T YOU DYING TO TAKE A BREAK?

I'M IYNGD FO THTRSI
I'M DYING OF THIRST!

EW CAN'T AFRODF THE PTIR.
WE CAN'T AFFORD THE TRIP.

I VHAE ON DNOCES HOTGSTUH.
I HAVE NO SECOND THOUGHTS.

TI WSA INDK OF A DRHA CNSIOIDE.
IT WAS KIND OF A HARD DECISION.

SHTI ZELZUP IS ROTS FO UFN.
THIS PUZZLE IS SORT OF FUN.

Secret Message:
IT TAKES TWO TO TANGO.
1 2 3 4 5 6 7 8 9 10 11 12 13 14 15 16 17

Lesson 2

As You Listen

- Annette is very tired because she didn't sleep last night. Also, she's worried about her grade on a quiz. She's under a lot of pressure.
- Yes, Alan is helpful. He listens to Annette and he tells her to go home and take a nap.

After You Listen

(A) T, ?, ?, F, ?

(B) **Guess the Meanings**

1. hit the books
2. hand in
3. pull an all-nighter
4. take a nap
5. in the nick of time

Your Turn: Listening Challenge

He's in hot water because he copied a few paragraphs from the Internet.

Script

I think I'm really in hot water with my teacher. She wrote a note on my paper that she wants to see me in her office tomorrow. I think I know why. I worked really hard on my last paper, but right before I had to hand it in, I got busy and I copied something from the Internet. Just a small thing. Maybe a few paragraphs. I didn't think she'd know. I can't believe it. I'm so scared. What will she do to me? I hope I don't get an F. What if she tells my parents? I'll be in really hot water with them, too. I promise to never copy again. I hope they'll believe me.

Exercises

1. Mini-dialogues

1A/B: d, f, e, g, j, a, i, b, c
2A/B: j, a, c, f, b, i, d, h, g

2. Grammar practice

1.b. a	2.a. on	3.a. crammed
1.c. the	2.b. in	3.b. stayed up
1.d. an	2.c. on	3.c. weren't
1.e. a	2.d. for	3.d. handed in
1.f. the	2.e. in . . . of	3.e. didn't turn in
	2.f. in	3.f. got
	2.g. in	3.g. hit
		3.h. didn't take

3. Error correction

1. My report was due yesterday, but I handed it in ~~it~~ today.
2. When the teacher handed ~~it~~ out the test, I was nervous.
3. I keep my teacher's handouts organized in my binder.
4. When the teacher hands back our tests, everyone looks worried. *OR:* When the teacher handed back our tests, everyone looked worried.
5. I need to turn in my homework. I don't want to turn it in late.
6. Great! I got an A!!!
7. When he was in his native country, he often took naps in the afternoon. *OR:* When he is in his native country, he often takes naps in the afternoon.
8. She hit the books ~~to study~~ last night.
9. I hope I do well on my next test.
10. When we were teenagers, every Saturday night we stayed up late.

4. Choosing the idiom

1. take a nap
2. stay up
3. pull an all-nighter
4. hit the books
6. turn it in/hand it in
7. be in hot water
8. doing well in
9. You can say that again

5. Sentence writing (Answers can vary.)

1. Joe usually **crams** the night before a test.
2. Sometimes he **pulls an all-nighter** before a test, so he's tired and his **mind goes blank.** (Sometimes he **stays up** all night before a test.) (When Joe has a test, he usually **stays up** late.)
3. Sometimes he **takes a test cold.**
4. When his teachers **hand out** tests, he gets really nervous.
5. He's even more nervous when they **hand back** tests.
6. Sometimes he **gets a D on a test.**
7. He **doesn't do well.**
8. Sometimes students **hand in** their homework.
9. Sometimes he does his homework **in the nick of time.**
10. His teachers tell him that he**'s in hot water** and that he needs to **hit the books.**
11. His **handouts** are very disorganized.
12. He needs to **take a nap** before he watches TV.

Lesson 3

As You Listen

- They're visiting so they can be together, relax, and watch some movies.
- No, they don't all agree about this.

After You Listen

(A) F, ?, T, T, T

(B) **Guess the Meanings**

1. get together
2. That makes two of us.
3. safe and sound
4. make yourselves comfortable
5. don't feel like

Your Turn: Listening Challenge

	(not) feel like ___ing	(not) be in the mood to ___
eat out/go dancing	• She feels like eating out and going dancing. • He doesn't feel like eating out and going dancing.	• She's in the mood to eat out and go dancing. • He isn't in the mood to eat out and go dancing.
stay home/watch TV	• She doesn't feel like staying home and watching TV. • He feels like staying home and watching TV.	• She isn't in the mood to stay home and watch TV. • He isn't in the mood to stay home and watch TV.
cook	• She doesn't feel like cooking.	• She isn't in the mood to cook.

Script

A: So, what do you feel like doing tonight?

B: Nothing. I just want to stay home. I need some peace and quiet.

A: Well, I'm in the mood to eat out and then go dancing.

B: I can't believe it! Where do you get your energy?

A: I don't know. I always feel like going out and doing something. And you just want to stay home and watch TV.

B: I want to stay home, but I didn't say anything about watching TV. I'm in the mood for a quiet, romantic dinner and maybe a movie. What do you think?

A: Sounds good, but who's going to cook? I don't feel like cooking. It's Friday night!

Exercises

1. Mini-dialogues

1A/B: e, a, b, h, d, i, c, g
2A/B: f, d, c, b, e, h, a

2. Grammar practice

1.a. with
1.b. for
1.c. at
1.d. in, for
1.e. in
1.f. of
1.g. on
1.h. with
1.i. at
1.j. for
2.a. getting/giving
2.b. taking
2.c. working
planting flowers
pulling weeds
3.a. the
3.b. a
4.a. got
4.b. made
4.c. was
4.d. felt
4.e. spent
5.a. outselves
5.b. myself
5.c. themselves
5.d. yourself
5.e. yourselves

3. Error correction

1. When they visit us, they always make themselves ~~comfortable~~ at home. *OR:* When they visit us, they always make themselves comfortable ~~at home~~.
2. I'm in a good mood ~~to go out tonight~~. *OR* I'm in the ~~good~~ mood to go out tonight.
3. I'm in the mood for ~~go to~~ a movie. *OR* I'm in the mood to go to a movie.
4. She feels like going to a movie.
5. He's in a very good mood today.
6. She never feels like spending time on her homework.
7. Last night, they spent two hours doing their homework.
8. We got together with them and took a long walk last Sunday.
9. They were (*OR:* are) safe and sound after their long trip.
10. Thanks for coming to my party.

4. Choosing the idiom

1. feel like
2. spend all my time
3. in the mood to
4. That makes two of us
5. get together
6. spend more time with
7. in the mood for

5. Sentence writing (Answers can vary.)

1. Dan always **spends time at** his computer.
2. For half the day, he **spends time searching** the Internet.
3. After he makes coffee, he **makes himself comfortable** and turns on his computer.
4. He's **in a bad mood** before he has some caffeine.
5. Sometimes Ann **feels like moving out** and **getting** her own apartment.
6. When Ann **is in the mood for** chicken, Dan **is in the mood for** steak.
7. When Ann **is in the mood to go** to the movies, Dan **is in the mood to stay** home.
8. When Ann wants to **get together with** her friends, Dan wants her to stay home.

9. Word search

M O O D R D V F T N L O O U R

Y K O K Y O U R S E L F I N E

V N S W M R U D E G R R A W T

X C J E S G N I V A H F W N E

N H D L E G N I T T I S O T U

E W V N E S E V L E S R U O Y

Q G F B I D L I H B P T S O S

K O A R N D D X U F B O U X O

R T S E G M S O L Q O E X K R

M M Y J O J N R Z V G R X I M

B C O M I N G P G K T D Y D A

W J A E H T M D S N B J N C K

J E S O U N D T K N O Q N U E

Y B B R F H X M G Z F A P E S

K R B M A Y S A E L G Q B R N

Lesson 4

As You Listen

- The problem is that there's a really big blackout in about five states.
- Dave got the information online.

After You Listen

(A) T, T, ?, F, T

(B) **Guess the Meanings**

1. chances are
2. in charge of
3. be over
4. looks like
5. go out of my mind

Your Turn: Listening Challenge

1. They're working on the problem of homelessness/ending homelessness/helping homeless people.
2. He's working on getting better/higher grades/improving his grades/getting As.
3. She's working on getting emergency supplies/preparing for an emergency.

Script

1. It's a big problem and we need to solve it. But don't worry—we're working on it. Too many people are living on the streets. We're trying to help them. We're finding them places to live and helping them get jobs. And, of course, we have people helping them with their drug and alcohol problems. Please know that we're doing all we can. We're working on this day and night.

2. Dad, I know, I know. Yeah, it's true that I didn't work very hard and that's why my grades were so bad. But I've changed. Right now I'm working on two papers and I know I'm doing a good job. And I had a big test last week and do you know how long I studied? Six hours a day for three days! Really—believe me—this time I'm going to get all As. Don't worry.

3. Last week, there was a really big storm that started in the evening and lasted all night. The electricity went out and we had a terrible flood. We had a lot of water on the first floor of our house, so we had to stay upstairs. We had a flashlight, but after about an hour, the batteries died, so we lit some candles. Our cell phones didn't work and we didn't have a radio to find out what was going on, so it was really scary. So today, guess where I'm going? That's right, I'm going shopping. And I'm going to get flashlights, batteries, and a radio or two. Maybe I should check the Internet to get a good list of emergency supplies.

Exercises

1. Mini-dialogues

1 A/B: c, a, g, f, b, d
2 A/B: d, g, a, b, f, c

2. Grammar practice

1.a. for
1.a. in, of
1.b. on
1.c. in
1.d. of
1.e. of
1.f. on

3.a. was
3.b. will be/are going to be
3.c. am
3.d. was
3.e. was/went
3.f. were, weren't
3.g. is
3.h. was/went

2.a. getting/buying/preparing
2.b. getting
2.c. thinking/dreaming

3. Error correction

1. I'm finished (done) with my homework.
2. Chances are that the weather will be better tomorrow.
3. I went out of my mind with all that work last week.
4. When the power came back on at 5 o'clock, everyone clapped.
5. When I asked him what he was doing, he said he was working on his application.
6. We're in the dark about that. Tell us what happened.
7. He's only 12, but he ~~looks~~ sounds just like his father on the phone.
8. They didn't call to say they were late, so we went out of our minds worrying about them.
9. It sounds like you had a great vacation.
10. We got in (on) line at the bus stop.

4. Choosing the idiom

1. was going out of my mind
2. be in charge of
3. it sounds like
4. I sure am
5. am in the dark about
6. Chances are
7. got online
8. were afraid of the dark
9. it looks like
10. is over

5. Sentence writing (Answers can vary.)

1. Sophie and her friends **are working on** getting earthquake supplies.
2. Sophie **is in charge** because she's the oldest.
3. **It looks like** this is a lot of work.
4. **Chances are**, they'll be finished in a day or two.
5. When they started, they **were in the dark about** what supplies to get.
6. But they **got online** and found a Web site with information.
7. Sophie **was going out of her mind** because the discount store was so crowded.
8. It **sounds like** a lot of work.
9. Are the teachers and parents happy to have their help? **They sure are!**

9. Unscramble and find the secret message

WOH'S NI AEGRHC RHEE?
WHO'S IN CHARGE HERE?

I RESU MA!
I SURE AM!

WE ESRU ERA!
WE SURE ARE!

LET'S EGT ONINLE AT AN TTENERIN ACFE.
LET'S GET ONLINE AT AN INTERNET CAFE.

IT SOOLK KELI WE SEMDIS ETH BUS.
IT LOOKS LIKE WE MISSED THE BUS.

SHE KSOOL KILE HER RSITES.
SHE LOOKS LIKE HER SISTER.

TI SDSNOU LIEK UOY DHA FUN.
IT SOUNDS LIKE YOU HAD FUN.

UYO SDNUO ELKI EM.
YOU SOUND LIKE ME.

OYU NUOSD ILEK UOY EHAV A OCDL.
YOU SOUND LIKE YOU HAVE A COLD.

EH SEEDN OT RWOK ON IHS KMOWHERO.
HE NEEDS TO WORK ON HIS HOMEWORK.

I SWA NI EHT RDAK BUTOA TATH!
I WAS IN THE DARK ABOUT THAT!

CESHACN RAE HTE TSOMR IWLL EB ERVO OSON.
CHANCES ARE THE STORM WILL BE OVER SOON.

I'M SO BORED, I'M IGGNO OUT OF MY MNID.
I'M SO BORED, I'M GOING OUT OF MY MIND.

OND'T WROK NI HET KADR.
DON'T WORK IN THE DARK.

Secret Message:

IT'S BETTER TO BE SAFE THAN SORRY!

Lesson 5

As You Listen

- They are a mother and daughter.
- The problem is that the mother says she has a lot of work that will prevent her from going out to dinner on her birthday. The final decision is that she'll work longer hours so she can get her work done and be free on Thursday evening.

After You Listen

(A) T, T, F, ?, ?

(B) **Guess the Meanings**

1. take you up on
2. talk you into
3. going back and forth
4. through with
5. take a rain check

Your Turn: Listening Challenge

1. Sam is going back and forth about helping his community or traveling.
2. Ann is going back and forth between two restaurants for her husband's retirement party.

Script

1. Well, I have some news for you. After working hard for over 40 years, I just retired. Everyone congratulates me and I'm glad I don't have to wake up early every morning to go to work. But I have a problem—I need to decide what to do with myself every day. I'm driving my wife crazy. The problem is, I keep changing my mind. One day I think I should volunteer at a school near where I live—maybe help a kid learn to read. You know, I want to make a difference and help out in my community. Then the next day, I want to travel and just enjoy myself. I go back and forth about what to do and I'm still not doing anything. Oh—here's my wife. She wants to talk to you.

2. Hi there. Now it's my turn. I've been retired for a few years now, and I have no problem deciding what to do with my days. Between helping out with the grandkids and going out with my friends, I'm having a great time. And I'm really enjoying planning my husband's retirement party. He doesn't know I'm doing this. Anyway, our house is too small for a party like that, so I looked at some restaurants with one of my friends. I really like two of the restaurants. One is on the beach and it has a great view. And my husband loves the beach. But it's far from here. Another is right in the city so it's easy to get to, and it has great food. It's really famous, but it's a little noisy. Every minute I go back and forth between these two places. I don't know. Maybe I should just tell my husband what I'm planning and he can decide.

Exercises

1. Mini-dialogues

1A/B: c, e, d, b, h, a, f
2A/B: g, d, f, a, e, b, h

2. Grammar practice

1.a. with
1.b. in
1.c. to/in
1.d. to
1.e. into
1.f. of
1.g. in
1.h. between
1.i. about
1.j. to
1.k. with

2.a. making
2.b. getting/buying
2.c. taking/accepting
2.d. visiting/seeing
2.e. cleaning

3.a. weren't
3.b. didn't make
3.c. didn't get
3.d. didn't go
3.e. wasn't

3. Error correction

1. I'm looking forward to seeing you.
2. When you're through with cleaning your room, can you clean mine?

3. When they were through with dinner, they watched TV.
4. I didn't know what to do. I kept going back and forth between taking four classes and five classes.
5. A: Where should we go on Sunday?
   B: I have two ideas in ~~my~~ mind.
6. They were going to go skiing when the roads were bad, and luckily we talked them out of going.
7. He needed to have a serious conversation with his brother, and now he feels better because he got it over with.
8. We're sorry we can't come over tonight. Can we take a rain check for next Friday?
9. After the hurricane, the city was swamped with donations.
10. It makes no difference if you come tomorrow instead of today.

4. Choosing the idiom

1. have in mind
2. am drowning
3. talk you out of
4. am through with
5. going back and forth
6. talked me into
7. am looking forward to/look forward to
8. After all

5. Sentence writing (Answers can vary.)

1. Jerry **was swamped with** work.
2. Whenever anyone asked him to go to the movies or out to dinner, he always **asked for a rain check.**
3. He stayed at work late because he kept saying, "I'll **get one more thing over with.**"
4. **It didn't make a difference** if he was sick. He still went to work.
5. Every day, he **looked forward to going** to work.
6. When his family told him he needed help, he asked them what they **had in mind.**
7. He kept **going back and forth about** getting some help.
8. His son **talked him into making** an appointment.
9. Now he's **through with being** a workaholic.
10. He spends more time with his family and friends. **After all**, they are the most important people in his life.

9. Word search

P	B	G	A	G	H	R	L	W	V	D	V	P	D	K
N	T	M	N	B	Y	R	U	O	B	R	Y	K	R	I
A	A	U	B	I	R	T	P	X	I	S	B	X	X	U
F	K	A	Q	T	N	J	B	Q	N	B	V	J	P	A
T	E	N	R	H	B	W	K	D	W	B	F	L	R	S
E	Y	J	N	R	X	C	O	F	G	H	X	L	J	X
R	F	M	C	O	K	Y	V	R	O	O	Z	V	U	O
Z	D	N	S	U	R	F	M	Z	D	R	T	H	I	C
O	E	L	P	G	F	O	I	U	A	E	W	T	L	E
L	K	R	W	H	Y	P	N	N	M	D	J	A	H	R
V	L	X	A	G	T	A	D	O	Y	F	G	N	R	T
M	A	J	P	M	Z	A	E	P	Q	F	O	W	S	D
J	T	K	G	Z	Z	N	A	F	Q	Y	I	R	Z	J
R	X	A	E	C	N	E	R	E	F	F	I	D	T	R
A	D	A	D	P	H	I	Y	H	Y	J	W	R	R	H

Lesson 6

As You Listen

- They are old friends.
- They talk about their families.

After You Listen

(A) T, T, F, ?, T

(B) **Guess the Meanings**

1. in ages
2. down the road
3. ran into you
4. You're kidding!
5. it turned out that

Your Turn: Listening Challenge

1. Gabriela fell down when she was on her way to the bus stop.
2. When they arrived, it was hard for the paramedics to get to Gabriela because so many students were standing around her. The students were in the way.
3. Gabriela's classmate drove her home even though her apartment was out of his way.
4. Gabriela put her leg on the back seat when they were on their way to her place.

Script

I have a story to tell you. What a day I had! Well, I was on my way to the bus stop after class when I fell down in the hallway. I hurt my leg and someone called an ambulance because I couldn't get up or walk. A lot of students were standing in a circle around me, and I was really nervous and in pain. When the paramedics came, they told everyone to move because they were in the way. I felt very important.

The good news was that the paramedics told me that my leg wasn't broken, and they helped me get up. Wow—did it hurt! Luckily, one of my classmates offered to drive me home. I thanked him and told him it was out of his way because we live on opposite sides of town, but he told me that he was happy to drive me home. On our way to my place, I sat in the back seat of the car, so I could put my leg on the seat. It really hurt. But the good thing is that now my classmate is my new friend. So, you see, when you wake up in the morning, you never know what will happen. And if something bad happens, sometimes something good can happen, too. Right?

Exercises

1. Mini-dialogues

1A/B: b, d, c, e, f, g
2A/B: c, a, g, f, b, d

2. Grammar practice

1.a. for
1.b. in
1.c. on
1.d. with
1.e. of
1.f. into
1.g. in
1.h. on
1.i. of
1.j. with

2.a. us
2.b. you
2.c. him/her/them
2.d. us

3.a. kept
3.b. caught
3.c. ran

3. Error correction

1. I think I lost my cell phone when I was on my way to class.
2. All that homework keeps (*OR:* kept) me busy.
3. Toys keep the children busy.
4. I like history, but the rest of my family loves science.
5. Don't worry. Nothing bad happened. I was kidding.
6. She hasn't visited him in ages.
7. We expected the test to be hard, but it turned out to be easy.
8. I waited for you for ages, but then I left. I didn't know what to do.
9. When she described her job, her friend said, "It sounds too good to be true."
10. Down the road, I'm sure you'll be (*OR:* you're going to be) a big success.

4. Choosing the idiom

1. in ages
2. believe it or not
3. You're kidding
4. for ages
5. in my way
6. run into
7. catch up on
8. the rest of

5. Sentence writing

Hi! You know me. I'm Sue. I know we haven't talked **in ages** and you said that you want to **catch up on** my news. Well, **believe it or not**, I'm not a vegetarian anymore. I know you think **I'm kidding**, but I'm not. Maybe I'll change again **down the road**. Who knows?

Well anyway, I'm sure you want to know **the rest of** my news. Listen to this! When I was at a restaurant with my friend Martin last week, I thought I saw our English teacher. I was scared, but I went over to her table to say hello. When I got there, **it turned out not to be** our teacher (*OR:* **it turned out that she wasn't our teacher**). I was really embarrassed, as you can imagine.

There isn't much else to talk about. I **keep busy** with schoolwork and my part-time job. And I'm applying to college.

I know I've been talking to you **for ages** and you need to go. Thanks for listening!

esson 7

As You Listen

- The problem is that Michael is upset that Kathy is throwing bottles away and not recycling them.
- They all will take some bottles home and recycle them there.

After You Listen

(A) F, T, ?, ?, F

(B) **Guess the Meanings**

1. go through
2. found out
3. take out
4. cared about
5. hold it

Your Turn: Listening Challenge

Alice	• found a great Web site about Japan	• found out about customs in India • needs to find out about customs in Ethiopia, Japan, and Peru
Mark	• found Alice in the library	• found out what he doesn't want to do research on • found out that he doesn't want to do research on classical music • found out that he wants to do research on the history of jazz

Script

1. Hi! I'm Alice. I'm doing some Internet research on wedding customs in four different countries. I already found out a lot about customs in India, but I need to find out more about customs in Ethiopia, Japan, and Peru.
2. Hi! Remember me? I'm Alice. I just wanted to let you know that I found a great Web site with information about wedding customs in Japan. If you want me to e-mail you the address, just let me know.

3. Hi! I'm Mark. I'm in Alice's class and I have the same assignment. At first, I didn't know what topic to do research on. But I found Alice in the library and talked to her. She gave me some good ideas to think about. I'll let you know tomorrow what I decide to do research on.
4. Hi there! I finally made my decision! Sorry you had to wait, but I wanted to be sure I picked the right research topic. As you know, yesterday I talked to Alice about a few possible topics. And then, I got online and looked at a few Web sites. First, I found out what I *don't* want to do research on, and that's classical music because I already know a lot about that. Well, after looking at a lot of Web sites, I decided to do research on the history of jazz because I don't know anything about that.

Exercises

1. Mini-dialogues

1A/B: d, f, h, i, e, a, c
2A/B: e, h, g, a, i, c, b, d

2. Grammar practice

1.a. of	2.a. learning
1.b. off	2.b. going
1.c. through	2.c. eating
1.d. of	
1.e. on	3.e. couldn't
1.f. about	3.f. got
1.g. about	3.a. went/threw
1.h. of	3.b. took
1.i. in	3.c. ran
1.j. on	3.d. found/did/felt
1.k. of	
1.l. after	

3. Error correction

1. I did a lot of research when I was a student.
2. They're very busy because they take care of their children and their elderly parents.
3. Every Saturday, I clean ~~up~~.
4. After the party, I cleaned up.
5. We found ~~out~~ a good article in the newspaper.
6. What on earth is going on here?
7. I need to find out where he is going.
8. He has a lot of old clothes and he wants to throw them away.
9. They felt guilty because they forgot my birthday.
10. She took all of her clothes out of her closet.

4. Choosing the idiom

1. What in the world	5. take care of
2. can't believe my eyes	6. care about
3. throw away	7. feel guilty
4. are running out of	8. find out about

5. Sentence writing (Answers can vary.)

1. Mike has a lot of stuff to **throw away (get rid of)**.
2. When he looked in his closet, he **felt guilty about** all the money he wasted on clothes that he never wore.
3. When he **was going through** his shirts, he found one or two that he liked.
4. When he **took them out of** his closet, he was surprised.
5. His mom **couldn't believe her eyes.**
6. She's glad he's finally **getting rid of things—throwing them away** or donating them.
7. She told him that he has to **take care of** his clothes.
8. Mike needs to search the Internet to **find out where** he can take his donations.

9. Unscramble and find the secret message

WHAT ON HEATR ARE OUY OINDG?
WHAT ON EARTH ARE YOU DOING?

I NAC'T VIBLEEE YM AERS!
I CAN'T BELIEVE MY EARS!

EHS DUONF UTO OHW NLEEADC PU.
SHE FOUND OUT WHO CLEANED UP.

EW ARN OTU OF IETM.
WE RAN OUT OF TIME.

TLE'S GO UGROHTH HET SETT GNIAA.
LET'S GO THROUGH THE TEST AGAIN.

EH OKTO HER CRUTPEI TUO OF SIH ELWALT.
HE TOOK HER PICTURE OUT OF HIS WALLET.

YHTE EACR A LOT TUBOA CAHE HETRO.
THEY CARE A LOT ABOUT EACH OTHER.

HYET KTEA CARE OF CEAH OHETR.
THEY TAKE CARE OF EACH OTHER.

OUY EWHRT YWAA MY SAENJ.
YOU THREW AWAY MY JEANS?

EW ELFE IGULTY UATBO ATHT.
WE FEEL GUILTY ABOUT THAT.

HTWA NI TEH LORDW RAE OYU NGNISGI?
WHAT IN THE WORLD ARE YOU SINGING?

ELT'S DO AREESRCH NO MISDOI.
LET'S DO RESEARCH ON IDIOMS.

Secret Message:
THE FIRST REAL RECYCLING PROGRAM WAS INTRODUCED IN NEW YORK CITY IN THE 1890S.

Lesson 8

As You Listen

- They are talking about what they are going to do over the break.
- They are talking about this because this is their last class.

After You Listen

(A) F, T, ?, T, T

(B) **Guess the Meanings**

1. far in advance
2. above all
3. show around
4. That's music to my ears!
5. get a lot out of something

Your Turn: Listening Challenge

Situation	Did it work out?	Why or why not?
1. summer camp last year	No.	It didn't work out because they didn't need him. There weren't enough kids.
2. getting married	No.	It didn't work out because they disagreed about a lot of things.
3. car/truck	Yes.	It worked out because she wanted a small car and he wanted a truck.

Script

1. Girl: What're you going to do over the summer?
   Boy: I'm going to be a camp counselor. Last year I was going to be a counselor at a camp about three hours from here, but it didn't work out.
   Girl: What happened?
   Boy: They didn't have enough kids and they didn't need me. I was really disappointed. So I'm happy I can be a counselor this year.
2. Woman: How was your honeymoon?
   Man: We didn't get married.
   Woman: You're kidding! What happened?
   Man: I wanted a big wedding. She wanted a small wedding. I wanted to get a dog. She wanted a cat. Our relationship just didn't work out.
   Woman: I'm sorry to hear that. Listen, why don't you come over and visit sometime. I have a cute dog I want you to meet.
3. Man: I heard you bought Tom's car, and that he bought your truck.
   Woman: That's right. He wanted a truck, and I wanted a small car. It worked out great.

Exercises

1. Mini-dialogues

1A/B: d, a, f, b, e, c
2A/B: a, d, f, b, c

2. Grammar practice

1.a. on
1.b. over
1.c. of
1.d. in
1.e. of
1.f. of
1.g. in
1.h. to
1.i. at
1.j. with
1.k. without
1.l. in
1.m. around

2.a. got
2.b. lost
2.c. were
2.d. were
2.e. showed
2.f. didn't work

3. Error correction

1. What are you going to do <u>over</u> the break?
2. People <u>were</u> better off a long time ago.
3. He got a lot out <u>of</u> his music class.
4. We wanted to go, but it didn't <u>work</u> out.
5. I plan to show <u>my friends</u> around the city.
6. They were out <u>of</u> touch for a long time, but they're back in touch now.
7. Be sure to be here ahead <u>of</u> time.
8. I'm so glad to hear that. <u>That's</u> music to my ears!
9. What do you usually do <u>on</u> weekends?
10. She <u>works</u> out three times a week.

4. Choosing the idiom

1. over the break
2. show me around
3. didn't work out
4. At least
5. work out
6. am better off
7. keep in touch with
8. got a lot out of
9. above all

5. Sentence writing

Hi everyone! Congratulations on finishing, or almost finishing, this book! I hope you **got a lot out of it**. And if you're going to have a test soon, I hope you **study in advance**!

When you finish your English course, maybe you're going to have a break. I hope that **over your break**, you'll get some rest. If you're not going to travel or do anything special, **at least** you'll have some free time.

I also hope that you're planning to **keep in touch with** some of your classmates. Maybe you'll email and call each other. And maybe some of you will visit each other and **show each other around**. If you do, I hope you'll communicate in English and use some of the expressions you learned. If I ever hear you use any of these expressions, I'll say, **"That's music to my ears!"**

Good luck as you continue to learn English. Keep paying attention to idioms and other expressions. They make a language more interesting. And **above all**, as you study English, have confidence in yourself and have a good time!

Review Answer Key

Lessons 1 and 2

1. get cold feet
2. calm down
3. pull an all-nighter
4. be kind of nervous
5. be just about ready to go
6. be dying to go
7. do well on a test
8. be there in the nick of time
9. for good
10. Hand in your report.
11. be in hot water
12. be sort of crazy
13. had second thoughts
14. My mind went blank.
15. call off the picnic
16. get a B on a test
17. couldn't afford to buy a house
18. take naps
19. hit the books
20. stay up past midnight

Lessons 3 and 4

1. Make yourself at home.
2. Help yourselves to a drink.
3. work on an application
4. get together and have lunch
   (*OR:* get together around 11:00)
5. be in the mood to watch TV
6. be in the mood for a cup of hot tea
7. smell like smoke
8. be in a very bad mood
9. feel like taking a nap
10. spent time thinking about that
11. Thanks for having me over.
12. safe and sound
13. be sound asleep
14. We sure are!
15. It looks like it's going to be impossible.
16. be afraid of the dark
17. be in charge of hiring
18. be over around 11:00
19. go out of your mind working on an application
20. go nuts

Lessons 5 and 6

1. swamped with work
2. drowning in work
3. Please give me a rain check.
4. It makes no difference where we go.
5. She talked us into driving.
6. That's what I had in mind.
7. for ages
8. It turned out to be great.
9. down the road
10. caught up with old friend
11. be through with working in the garden
12. run into them
13. Let's get this over with.
14. the rest of the day
15. go back and forth
16. in my way
17. look forward to relaxing.
18. He talked me into cooking.
19. They keep me busy.
20. believe it or not

Lessons 7 and 8

1. feel guilty about forgetting
2. be guilty of a serious crime
3. pay your bills in advance
4. run out of sugar
5. get a lot out of that course
6. What in the world is going on?
7. Let me show you around.
8. care about doing a good job
9. do research on butterflies
10. I hope it'll work out for you.
11. That's music to my ears!
12. go through your notes
13. get here ahead of time
14. Take your hand out of the cookie jar!
15. be better off changing our plans
16. get rid of that garbage
17. Take care of yourself!
18. Let's keep in touch!
19. At least it's not raining.
20. Clean up after the party.

Crossword Puzzle Solutions

Lessons 1 and 2

Lessons 5 and 6

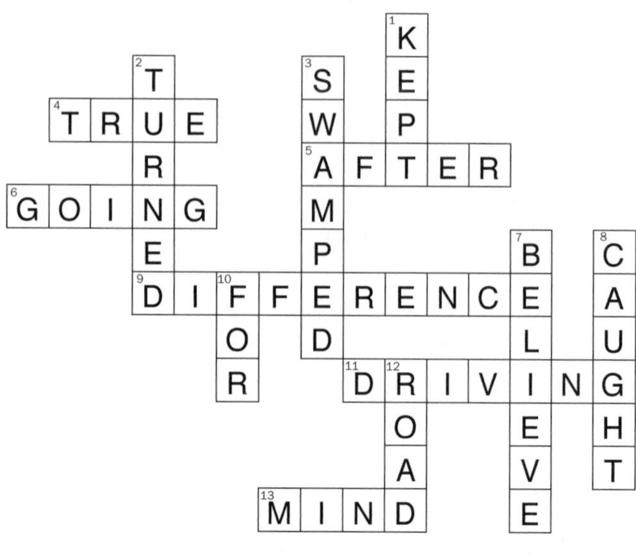

Lessons 3 and 4

Lessons 7 and 8

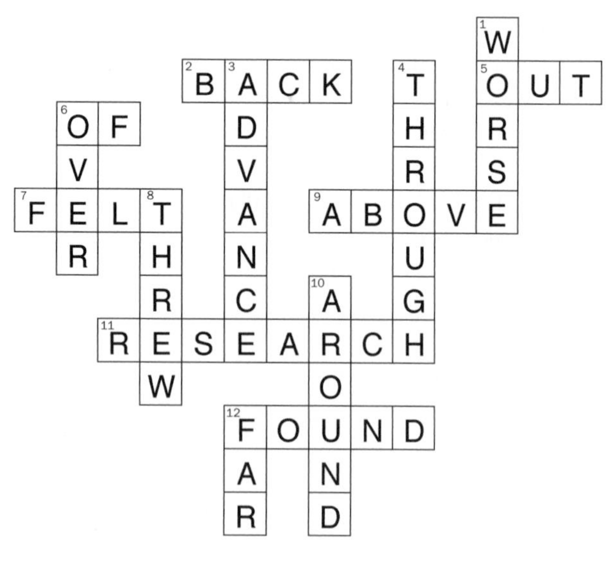

Pronunciation Answer Key

Lesson 7

Practice 1

Base form of regular verb	Final sound	Past tense	Final *-ed* sound
1. believe	/v/	believed	/t/ **/d/** /ɪd/
2. notice	/s/	noticed	**/t/** /d/ /ɪd/
3. try	/aɪ/	tried	/t/ **/d/** /ɪd/
4. help	/p/	helped	**/t/** /d/ /ɪd/
5. care	/r/	cared	/t/ **/d/** /ɪd/
6. want	/t/	wanted	/t/ /d/ **/ɪd/**
7. start	/t/	started	/t/ /d/ **/ɪd/**
8. happen	/n/	happened	/t/ **/d/** /ɪd/
9. need	/d/	needed	/t/ /d/ **/ɪd/**
10. ask	/k/	asked	**/t/** /d/ /ɪd/

Practice 2

Michael, Kathy, and Lee were cleaning up after a meeting when Michael suddenly noticed /t/ that Kathy was throwing a glass bottle away. He started /ɪd/ yelling because she wasn't recycling and he asked /t/ her if she cared /d/ about the environment. He talked /t/ about what he learned /d/ when he did some research on the lack of places for garbage, and this made Kathy feel guilty.

Lee suggested /ɪd/ that they all go through the garbage bags and take out the bottles. She offered /d/ to take them home and recycle them. But they decided /ɪd/ that all three of them would take bottles home. They agreed /d/ that this was the best thing to do.

Lesson 8

Practice 1

Singular noun	Final sound	Plural noun	Final *-s* sound		
1. week	/k/	weeks	**/s/**	/z/	/ɪz/
2. friend	/d/	friends	/s/	**/z/**	/ɪz/
3. ticket	/t/	tickets	**/s/**	/z/	/ɪz/
4. price	/s/	prices	/s/	/z/	**/ɪz/**
5. break	/k/	breaks	**/s/**	/z/	/ɪz/
6. job	/b/	jobs	/s/	**/z/**	/ɪz/
7. plan	/n/	plans	/s/	**/z/**	/ɪz/
8. movie	/i/	movies	/s/	**/z/**	/ɪz/
9. parent	/t/	parents	**/s/**	/z/	/ɪz/
10. exercise	/z/	exercises	/s/	/z/	**/ɪz/**
11. gym	/m/	gyms	/s/	**/z/**	/ɪz/
12. card	/d/	cards	/s/	**/z/**	/ɪz/

Practice 2

Base form of verb	Final sound	Third person singular form	Final *-s* sound		
1. ask	/k/	asks	**/s/**	/z/	/ɪz/
2. show	/oʊ/	shows	/s/	**/z/**	/ɪz/
3. wait	/t/	waits	**/s/**	/z/	/ɪz/
4. sound	/d/	sounds	/s/	**/z/**	/ɪz/
5. work	/k/	works	**/s/**	/z/	/ɪz/
6. happen	/n/	happens	/s/	**/z/**	/ɪz/
7. get	/t/	gets	**/s/**	/z/	/ɪz/
8. stay	/eɪ/	stays	/s/	**/z/**	/ɪz/
9. look	/k/	looks	**/s/**	/z/	/ɪz/
10. take	/k/	takes	**/s/**	/z/	/ɪz/
11. visit	/t/	visits	**/s/**	/z/	/ɪz/
12. keep	/p/	keeps	**/s/**	/z/	/ɪz/
13. practice	/s/	practices	/s/	/z/	**/ɪz/**
14. relax	/ks/	relaxes	/s/	/z/	**/ɪz/**
15. hope	/p/	hopes	**/s/**	/z/	/ɪz/

Practice 3

/ɪz/ /s/ /z/ /z/
When English classes end, it is common for students and their teachers to talk about their plans
/s/ /s/ /s/ /z/ /s/ /z/
during their breaks. Some students take trips and others stay home. Sometimes students have visitors
/s/ /z/ /z/
and they show them around. And some students work because their vacations from their jobs are
/z/
different from their school vacations.

/z/ /s/ /z/ /ɪz/ /ɪz/
My friend's brother never takes vacations. The only time he relaxes is when he watches TV.
/s/ /ɪz/ /ɪz/ /z/
He works almost all the time. When he has free time, he washes his car and fixes things around his house.
/ɪz/
And I know he exercises every day at the gym.

As for me, well, I always find time to relax!

Index: Alphabetical List of Idioms and Expressions

The blue number refers to the lesson number(s). The black number refers to the page number.